Transforming Vocation

TRANSFORMATIONS
THE EPISCOPAL CHURCH IN THE 21ST CENTURY

Transforming Vocation

SAM PORTARO

CHURCH PUBLISHING
an imprint of Church Publishing Incorporated, New York

Unless otherwise indicated, all passages from the Hebrew scriptures
are from *Tanakh: A New Translation of the Holy Scriptures according to
the Traditional Hebrew Text.* © 1985 by the Jewish Publication
Society. Passages from the Christian scriptures are from the *New
Revised Standard Version* of the Bible. © 1989 by the Division of
Christian Education of the National Council of Churches of Christ
in the U.S.A. Used by permission. All rights reserved.

       Library of Congress Cataloging-in-Publication Data
Portaro, Sam Anthony.
  Transforming vocation / by Sam Portaro.
     p.   cm.
  Includes bibliographical references.
  ISBN 978-0-89869-586-1 (pbk.)
  1. Discernment (Christian theology). 2. Vocation (Christianity).
  3. Authority—Religious aspects—Christianity. 4. Episcopal Church.
  I. Title.
  BV4509.5.P65 2008
  248.4'83—dc22
                                         2007044609

Printed in the United States of America.

Cover design by Stefan Killen Design.
Study guide and interior design by Vicki K. Black.

Church Publishing, Incorporated
445 Fifth Avenue
New York, New York 10016
www.churchpublishing.com

       5   4   3   2   1

Contents

Series Preface vii

Acknowledgments ix

1. Why Am I Here? 1

2. How Did We Get Here? 23

3. God's Gift to the World. 50

4. Why Are *We* Here? 80

5. The *Whole* Church. 112

A Guide for Discussion. 135

Resources 141

Notes and Sources 147

a note from the publisher

This series emerged as a partnership between the Office of Mission of the Episcopal Church and Church Publishing, as a contribution to the mission of the church in a new century. We would like to thank James Lemler, series editor, for bringing the initial idea to us and for facilitating the series. We also want to express our gratitude to the Office of Mission for two partnership grants: the first brought all the series authors together for two creative days of brainstorming and fellowship; and the second is helping to further publicize the books of the series to the clergy and lay people of the Episcopal Church.

Series Preface

B e ye transformed" (KJV). "Be transformed by the renewing of your minds" (NRSV). "Fix your attention on God. You'll be changed from the inside out" (*The Message*). Thus St. Paul exhorted the earliest Christian community in his writing to the Romans two millennia ago. This exhortation was important for the early church and it is urgent for the Episcopal Church to heed as it enters the twenty-first century. Be transformed. Be changed from the inside out.

Perhaps no term fits the work and circumstances of the church in the twenty-first century better than "transformation." We are increasingly aware of the need for change as we become ever more mission-focused in the life of the church, both internationally and domestically. But society as a whole is rapidly moving in new directions, and mission cannot be embraced in an unexamined way, relying on old cultural and ecclesiastical stereotypes and assumptions.

This new series, *Transformations: The Episcopal Church in the 21st Century*, addresses these issues in realistic and hopeful ways. Each book focuses on one area within the Episcopal Church that is urgently in need of transformation in order for the church to be effective in the twenty-first century: vocation, evangelism, preaching, congregational life, getting to know the Bible, leadership, Christian formation, worship, and stewardship. Each volume explains why a changed vision is essential, gives robust theological and biblical foundations, offers guidelines to best practices and positive trends, describes the necessary tools for change, and imagines how transformation will look.

In this volume Sam Portaro takes on the topic of vocation and identity in the Episcopal Church. Individuals and communities of faith require a strong sense of call, purpose, and identity for this new time. Vocational discernment brings clarity in a changing and sometimes confusing environment. How can communities and individuals discern a call from God within the vocations and tasks in which they find themselves? How can the church deal creatively with its confusion about the differing role and authority of ordained and lay ministers? Where are the seeds of transformation to be found? This is a serious concern for leaders, church members, and seekers alike.

Like Christians in the early church, today we live in a secular culture that can be apathetic and even hostile to Christianity. Living in a setting where people are not familiar with the message or narrative of Christian believing requires new responses and new kinds of mission for the Body of Christ. We believe this is a hopeful time for spiritual seekers and inquirers in the church. The gospel itself is fresh for this century. God's love is vibrant and real; God's mission can transform people's hopes and lives. Will we participate in the transformation? Will we be bearers and agents of transformation for others? Will we ourselves be transformed? This is the call and these are the urgent questions for the Episcopal Church in the twenty-first century.

But first, seek to be transformed. Fix your attention on God. You'll be changed from the inside out.

JAMES B. LEMLER,
series editor

Acknowledgments

While writing is often solitary, no author works alone. This book has drawn on many friendships and resources, only some of which are recalled and included here. At the outset I thank Cynthia Shattuck, under whose firm hand I have had the pleasure to write much and at whose behest I undertook this project. Jim Lemler and my companion authors in this series offered advice and encouragement, especially David Gortner, who made many helpful suggestions early on. For Vicki Black and the staff at Church Publishing who labor to bring my work to fulfillment I am deeply thankful.

Friends who read drafts are very dear, for they sacrifice time, suffer typographical errors, grammatical and syntactical snarls, and head-cramping leaps of logic and meaning, often responding with kindness, helpful insights, corrections, and always grace. Among them I thank Diana Butler Bass, Douglas Fenton, Don Frye, Michael Johnston, and Joyce Mercer. I particularly thank Diana Butler Bass and Joyce Mercer for valuable conversations that led to new resources and deeper reflection.

Mark Duffy at the Episcopal Church Archives and Mitzi Budde at the Bishop Payne Library of Virginia Theological Seminary responded quickly and efficiently to requests for information that greatly enhanced my memory and accuracy.

The congregations of the dioceses of Western North Carolina, Southern Virginia, and Chicago, especially Epiphany in Newton, North Carolina; Canterbury at William & Mary and Bruton Parish; and Brent House at The University of Chicago endured my own learning and formed me in ministry. They are abundantly present in these pages.

Conversations and consultations are a rich source of information and reflection. I am glad for the privilege of sampling the life of many communities and congregations, whose clergy and members have extended warm hospitality. Their names and locations are listed among the sources at the back of this book.

My colleagues and participants in CREDO, a wellness project of the Episcopal Church Pension Fund based in Memphis, Tennessee, have heard portions of this book in presentation and assisted with feedback and encouragement.

To all who generously allowed inclusion of their stories, with or without attribution, thank you.

My steadfast partner, Chris Dionesotes, has put up with frequent and long absences, fielded phone calls, and shielded from distractions. I thank God and his parents, George and Margaret, for him. Both of us rejoice in the opportunity to live more fully into our shared vocation of life together.

chapter one

Why Am I Here?

WANTED: Persons for a vocation that leads God's people in bearing witness to God's new creation revealed in Jesus Christ by the power of the Holy Spirit. Work schedule is shaped by relationships, focusing on what is important in people's lives, and depends on regular rhythms of work, rest and play. Compensation is shaped by a mutual discernment of what is necessary in order for the persons (and, where appropriate, their families) to have an appropriately well-lived life. The vocation involves cultivating holy dispositions, preaching and teaching, nurturing rigorous study and shaping practices of faithful living in church and world. Lifelong education and formation is expected in order to enable others also to grow throughout their lives. The successful candidate will collaborate with others toward the same ends. The person with this vocation reports to God.

— GREGORY JONES, "JOB DESCRIPTION,"
in The Christian Century *(10 January 2006)*

Vocational discernment has in some circles become nearly as lively an interest, and as nebulous a subject, as spirituality. And like spirituality, considerations of vocational discernment have tended toward a rather narrow treatment, suggesting that vocational discernment is limited to an elite or specialized few, and that those who undertake it are, or ought to be, set apart. Little consideration is given to vocational discernment outside the realm of ordained ministry in the church.

This book aims to encourage a renewed commitment to the ageless Christian discipline of vocational discernment as the foundation of all ministry, a discipline and responsibility of all the baptized, individually and collectively. With few exceptions, I have drawn most heavily upon the most reliable source I know, which is my own experience of more than thirty years in active ministry. Nearly all of those years were devoted to a campus ministry, a context aptly described by one former divinity school student as "a little laboratory" within which one can try things much more difficult to attempt in a parish. Those years also include a stint in a small mission congregation, its transition to self-supporting parish status, and six years as associate to the rector of a large, complex congregation with over one thousand members. Moreover, extensive supply and consulting work have allowed me to establish abiding relationships with a variety of congregations in the urban, small town, and rural communities of northern Illinois, and several states beyond.

Those experiences and relationships are used herein to frame, illustrate, or punctuate a text primarily aimed at stimulating consideration of and conversation about vocational discernment. These stories are frequently and intentionally cast without specific identification. By treating them generically, I emphasize that what distinguishes these stories are principles that are hardly unique to one place or parish and may be articulated in varied practices.

They are thus, like the parables of Jesus, more likely to provide a point of entry or identification for the reader. And they remind us that discernment is not imitation.

Discernment is an aspect of the Christian life and experience that pervaded my ministry to such an extent that it constitutes a significant portion of my own vocation. In *Inquiring and Discerning Hearts: Vocation and Ministry with Young Adults on Campus,* Gary Peluso and I identified vocational discernment as a significant and substantive portion of ministry on campus. In *Crossing the Jordan: Meditations on Vocation,* I reflected upon the life of Jesus and his vocational discernment revealed in scripture as a guide to contemplating our own vocational journeys.

This book, in returning to a subject so central to my own thought and ministry, allows me opportunity for greater scope. It reaches more deeply into Christian history, scripture, and experience, locating a biblical and theological foundation for vocation in Genesis. It likewise reaches farther than my previous work into Christian practice, expanding some of my learnings in campus ministry beyond that context to find application in congregations. Written in the first years of my retirement from the institutional responsibilities of ministry, this book has been shaped by my own discernment and transition into a new vocation in an ever-unfolding ministry. Though still very much an ordained priest, my daily life looks and feels more akin to that of the first order of ministry, the laity. I am aware once again that the boundaries of one's identity and vocation are more fluid than a more narrow interpretation of vocation would allow, and that the best laid plans are subject always to change. Vocation is boundless, freely traversing the categories of sacred and profane, church and world.

Wresting vocational discernment from its narrow and near exclusive confinement to professional ordained offices and restoring it to the whole church is a priority for ministry in and beyond the twenty-first century. For while there is precious little warrant in scripture for a church that gathers and keeps its members unto itself, there is abundant commission for a church which, through its scattered members and their varied gifts, extends to the farthest reaches the compelling love of God. Vocational discernment is not just how the institutional church finds its ordained leadership. Vocational discernment is the most basic and essential expression of the church's mission.

the big question

Experience has taught me that in any process of vocational discernment attention must first and always be paid to the BIG questions, which are really only ONE big question: *Why am I here?* This essential question has many dimensions. It can be posed in any moment and in every instance beckons the asker into deeper reflection even as it offers insight. It is cast in three dimensions—the three dimensions of human life in all its fullness:

+ Why did God make me? *(past)*

+ What am I to do with my life and love?
  How do I fit in here? *(present)*

+ What and where will I be tomorrow? *(future)*

What kind of work will I do, to whom will I commit my love, and what kind of shape and meaning will my life take? For Christians, the answers to these questions—and the journey to those answers—is the subject of some of our most fervent and sincere prayer. The journey to those answers takes us through our riskiest and richest relationships, animates our anxiety and our exhilaration, traverses our deepest sadness and our most substantive satisfactions.

Moreover, the natural processes of aging and maturation only renew and reshape these challenges, framing the questions within the changing context of our personal lives as the web of relationships and responsibilities grows. As I grow older, what meaningful work can I do, what shape and expression will my love take?

The church has a name for this process. It's called *vocational discernment.*

Vocation: from the Latin *vocatio,* "a calling"; *vocatus,* "to call"

Discernment, from the Latin *discernere, dis-,* "apart" + *cernere,* "separate"

Practically speaking, it means separating and setting apart the desires of God for my life from all the competing desires and demands thrust at and upon me. And sometimes, clarifying and embracing the challenge of diminished options.

Throughout the journey of vocational discernment we are accompanied by the big question of why I am here, but the question takes on a particular urgency when a poverty of possibilities leaves us stranded on an unfamiliar threshold. This was the case in my senior year of college, when my intention to pursue graduate study in English was dashed by President Nixon's order canceling all educational draft deferments except for students of medicine, dentistry, or ministry. Once the shock of this news settled into reality, I was plunged into an intense introspection, surfacing only on the rare occasion when in the company of friends in similar circumstances.

Pondering my fate, I set out on an aimless walk one afternoon and was soon lost in deep thought. My feet knew the campus well, so on I walked, like a human pointer on a cosmic Ouija board, giving no thought to destination. I had no clue where my life's path was tending except, perhaps, an early death in some distant Southeast Asian jungle. I was thus surprised to find myself in the rector's office at the Episcopal church, where for three and a half years I'd lurked in a pew pretty regularly on Sunday mornings. I was even more surprised to hear myself say, "I think I want to be a priest."

I have come in order that you might have life—life in all its fullness. *(John 10:10, Today's English Version)*

Suddenly my life was radically reoriented. With dizzying speed I was propelled into a new and totally unexpected future. Within six weeks I was confirmed. I hurtled through the postulancy process and a few short months later, I began seminary. Safe and secure in the notion that I had found my vocation, it was not long before all those hibernating impulses to control roused from slumber and moved back into action. But in the course of three years in seminary there were many occasions of challenge, confrontation, and change, and once again, on the brink of graduation a number of experiences brought the realization that I could not move forward. I went to my faculty advisor and then to my bishop and I closed the book on the ordination process.

The search for employment did not go well. The nation was in economic recession and all the logical leads to which I applied, like education and social services, deemed me overqualified, an assessment less flattering than frustrating. In desperation I turned to an employment agency and was astonished, and grateful, to be hired as corporate general manager of a family-owned women's wear retailer. Why, I asked the owner, was he hiring me? I had no experience to suggest any preparation—much less aptitude—for this position.

The answer he offered was simple. "Our previous manager had an MBA and was a promiscuous womanizer whose numerous affairs, some with employees, destroyed staff morale and, in turn, ruined our business. We've fired our entire management team and are starting fresh. We've just hired a new floor manager, a young woman with an undergraduate degree in religion and a certificate in fashion merchandising. We'd like you to be our general manager. We can teach you everything you need to know about this business in six weeks, but you can't teach a person how to be moral."

I did indeed learn much about the business in a few short weeks and discovered the pastoral dimensions of supervising and overseeing more than sixty employees and a complex organization. Then, just over a year into the job, I developed a near-fatal illness that left me literally all by myself, quarantined and flat on my back for days on end, providing ample opportunity to get deeply in touch with myself, and with God. Later I would find compelling parallels with the vocational discernment of Ignatius of Loyola, a sixteenth-century Basque noble who had been destined for a career in the military and nobility. His life was radically changed when a severe wound at the battle of Pamplona in 1521 ended his military career, and during his long and painful convalescence he struggled to discover what his heart's desire truly was.

> For Ignatius, discernment based on desire is not merely a method of making choices or decisions but becomes a way of describing the whole fabric of Christian life, both personal and collective. — *Philip Sheldrake*

Miraculously, I survived the illness. Nearly two years after graduation from seminary I went to my bishop. I did not ask to be ordained; I simply offered myself to the possibility. My first assignment was to a small mission congregation in a southern mill town whose major employer, a textile factory, had recently closed. In that post and every one that followed I discovered that in God's economy no experience is ever wasted. My brief hiatus in the retail world had completed my education and preparation for my ministry. I had learned and was called to use all I knew of financial management, public relations, promotion, and communications in service to the church. And the time eventually came when language and writing skills honed in college and integral to my work in management and ministry became a prominent part of my vocation. This dynamic process of vocational discernment is the heart of each believer's life journey, yet despite the foundational theology of the laity developed in recent decades, the church in the beginning of the twenty-first century offers few resources to assist any except those examining a call to ordained service.

orders of ministry reconsidered

Interest in a "theology of the laity" emerged in Europe after World War II, notably in the works of the Dutch Reformed scholar Hendrik Kraemer, the first director of the Ecumenical Institute in Bossey, Switzerland, whose *Theology of the Laity* appeared in 1958, and of the French Dominican Yves Marie Joseph Cardinal Congar, who published *Lay People in the Church: A Study for a Theology of the Laity* in the same year. Both men opened serious inquiry into the role and vocation of the laity in the mid-1950s and their work was succeeded and amplified in the 1960s by another Catholic scholar, Hans Urs von Balthasar. These three European theologians, two of them Roman Catholics whose influence was strongly felt in the work of the Second Vatican Council convened in 1962, pioneered a new consideration of lay life and vocation.

The changing nature of ministry and its orders has lifted the laity to new prominence and has at the same time prompted a reconsideration of the servanthood of the episcopal, presbyteral, and diaconal orders. Yet one more time in Christian history, in ways reminiscent of the sixteenth-century Protestant Reformation, after a long season (in some cases amounting to centuries) in which the laity toiled to raise edifices, salary administrators and sacramentalists, and support programs in a system that invited and encouraged their passive acquiescence to an agenda not their own, the tables are being turned.

At present, however, we are in the midst of the turning. As in any massive reformation, the middle state is marked more by chaos than not. The dismantling of old systems only partly done, and orderly transition into a new manner of living incomplete, we are still sorting what to discard, what to keep, what is sufficient, what is still needed. Hints do, however, emerge.

The revision of the American Book of Common Prayer in 1979 added a clearly articulated Baptismal Covenant that has become for many Episcopalians a helpful and clarifying expression of the baptized life. In this covenant we are asked to make these affirmations about the way we will live:

* Will you continue in the apostles' teaching and fellowship, in the breaking of bread, and in the prayers?

* Will you persevere in resisting evil, and, whenever you fall into sin, repent and return to the Lord?

* Will you proclaim by word and example the Good News of God in Christ?

* Will you seek and serve Christ in all persons, loving your neighbor as yourself?

* Will you strive for justice and peace among all people, and respect the dignity of every human being? (BCP 304–305)

With the Prayer Book's emphasis on baptism as a public rite, especially in the prominent celebrations of Easter and Pentecost, the Baptismal Covenant has become familiar to many. Its language is often repeated in sermons and makes its way into diocesan and parish mission statements. The notion and expression of "living into our baptism" are fairly common in Episcopal contexts. Yet while the concepts of baptismal promise and responsibility are more widely evident in such repetition, the practical reality suggests that the Episcopal Church has lagged in its provision of vocational discernment and support for and among the laity, the frontline laborers called and commissioned to bear the fullness of God in and to the world.

The canons of the Episcopal Church likewise point to a renewed appreciation for the ministry of the laity, the fullness of which the church has not yet lived into. It was not until 1988, for example, that the General Convention amended its canons on ministry even to acknowledge "the Ministry of All Baptized Persons," directing that "Each Diocese shall make provision for the development and affirmation of the ministry of all baptized persons in the Church and in the world." Another fifteen years (five triennial conventions) lapsed before canonical revisions mandated specific attention to resources for vocational discernment for the laity:

Canon 1: Of the Ministry of All Baptized Persons
Sec. 1. Each Diocese shall make provision for the affirmation and development of the ministry of all baptized persons, including:
(a) Assistance in understanding that all baptized persons are called to minister in Christ's name, to identify their gifts with the help of the Church and to serve Christ's mission at all times and in all places.
(b) Assistance in understanding that all baptized persons are called to sustain their ministries

through commitment to lifelong Christian formation.   (Title III, "Ministry")

Practically speaking, this means that dioceses and congregations are to devote energy and emphasis to the ministry of *each person,* and to provide resources to that end. It means that attention is to be given to educating each person at every stage of maturation, teaching each one that his/her life is given and valued by God as integral to the life and vitality of the world. Moreover, it means that encouragement and education is not a "program" but an expectation and an orientation consistent with the baptismal commitment to lifelong formation and discernment. Yet with few exceptions, in most dioceses individual vocational discernment is so construed that its only purpose and terminus is professional ordination, either to the diaconate or priesthood.

Consider the obvious imbalance in the precedence given to ordination in the process of canon revision. Since 1985 the canons for ordained ministry have been overhauled twice, each time requiring a massive deployment of time, imagination, and energy involving parish and diocesan committees and commissions. Previously, a person interested in testing a vocation to ordained ministry met only with the rector, then with the bishop and various bodies like the Commission on Ministry and the Standing Committee. Those committees advised the bishop, who held sole authority in the matter of who was to be ordained. Subsequent revisions have allowed congregations to establish "discernment committees" who meet with the aspirant over several months, even a year, and collaborate with the rector to determine whether the aspirant should be encouraged to persevere. If so, the aspirant is referred to the bishop, and then moves on to a host of similarly elaborate committees and conversations aimed at clarifying the individual's vocation. The complex canonical demands pertaining to ordination have often been met in a creative and timely manner. But in the main, no comparable effort has been given to provide the laity with assistance in clarifying their vocations, suggesting that ordained ministry is the tail wagging the dog of the church.

Q. Who are the ministers of the Church?
A. The ministers of the Church are lay persons, bishops, priests, and deacons. *(BCP 855)*

The laity are the first order of ministry, according to the Catechism of the 1979 Book of Common Prayer, but what does that mean? Although we might assume that this stated primacy would ensure the laity the best resources for identifying and implementing their gifts, that is seldom the case. So long as bishops, priests, and deacons continue to occupy the most visible roles in public religious leadership, with sophisticated discernment processes, distinctive vestments to mark their office, and elaborate rites to set them apart, the laity are relegated to a different (and, implied, lesser) status. Those seeking clarity in the call and commitment of their specific gifts to God's service are thus encouraged toward ordination, or left wanting.

the voice of the laity

Clearly, ordained and lay ministries are locked in competition for attention and resources, and thus far, the laity have been overshadowed. The Episcopal Church is hardly alone in its fixation on ordained leadership; the entire Christian church offers few exceptions to professional clergy leadership designated and distinguished by difference from the laity. Dependence upon this structural order, like many dependencies, is complicated.

Part of that complication derives from human nature, or what the church has traditionally called "sin." Simply put, we tend to be self-serving creatures who, in turn, tend to create self-serving institutions. The willingness of clergy to exercise authority, and the tendency of the laity to defer to that authority, in many instances led to a "Father (or Mother) knows best" attitude. Clergy were deemed "experts" like their professional counterparts in medicine and law; they were expected to articulate a vision for parish life and programming and to administer the parish much as any voluntary nonprofit agency might be run.

Few questioned an apparent contradiction in a system that allowed those described in scripture as "servants" (the community's leaders) to issue orders for the laity to carry out. Nor did many question a system clearly at odds with Jesus' assertion that all models of inequality predicated upon hierarchies (like master and servant) were to be supplanted by an equality and collegiality common to friendship.

> I do not call you servants any longer, because the servant does not know what the master is doing; but I have called you friends. (John 15:15)

Both clergy and laity were complicit in this reversal, as it served each equally well. For several generations the usually benign tyranny of clergy endured and the laity grew accustomed to an equally benign submission. Correcting this unbiblical role reversal has not been easy. From the 1960s onward, coincidental with declines in church membership, participation, and funding, and with the breakdown of similar inequalities like race and gender in the social sphere, some elected to abandon the church altogether. Unfortunately, with them went much of the very resistance most needed to engage and effect a reforming reversal of this inequality within the church. Many of those who stayed in the church remained committed to the old patterns of relationship. Even when and where clergy willingly undertook to challenge the imbalance and change the relationship, the laity were unsure, or unwilling, to take up responsibility. Typical is an example from my own experience. I was a member of a diocesan commission delegated to implement a 1976 General Convention mandate to study issues of human sexuality. Dispatched one evening in 1977 to lead a parish discussion, I had completed my initial presentation and we were in the question-and-answer session, which zeroed in on the hot-button topic, homosexuality. I called upon a rather agitated gentleman some years my senior who had been impatiently waiting his turn. With considerable edge in his voice, he asked brusquely, "What I want to know is when is the church going to tell us where it stands on this issue?" To which I replied, perhaps a bit too testily myself, "I don't know, sir. When are you going to tell us? Last time I checked, you are as much a part of 'the church' as any of us here."

Such examples are diminishing. In the intervening years the voices of lay people have been accorded greater opportunity and respect. Notable among the Episcopal contributors is William Stringfellow, a lawyer who lived a simple life in service to the poor and wrote several insightful books, including *A Private and Public Faith*, in which he said, "For lay folk in the Church . . . there is no forbidden work. There is no corner of human existence, however degraded or neglected, into which they may not venture; no person, however beleaguered or possessed, whom they may not befriend and represent; no cause, however vain or stupid, in which they may not witness; no risk, however costly or imprudent, which they may not undertake."[1]

Stringfellow's near contemporary and fellow Washingtonian, Verna Dozier, was a high school English teacher who was widely respected for her teaching of scripture and for "claiming" the authority of the laity. "The Church of God is all the people of God," she wrote:

> lay and ordained, each order with its unique vocation, the lay order to be the people of God in the world, to witness by their choices and their values, in the kingdoms of the world, in the systems of commerce and government, education and medicine, law and human relations, science and exploration, art and vision, to witness to all these worlds that there is another possibility for human life than the way of exploitation and domination; and the vocation of the ordained order is to serve the lay order, to refresh and restore the weary souls with the Body and the Blood, to maintain those islands, the institutional church, where life is lived differently but always in order that life may be lived differently everywhere.[2]

Opportunities for theological education in formats and locations accessible to lay people have also proliferated. The popular Church's Teaching Series, six volumes for lay education developed by the Episcopal Church first in the 1950s, rewritten and published in a new edition of seven volumes in the late 1970s, and most recently revamped by yet a different set of authors in the late 1990s, did much to enrich lay education and prepare the way for more substantial curricula, including Education for Ministry. Commonly known to Episcopalians as EFM, this program, begun in 1975 by the School of Theology of the University of the South, encompasses a four-year study of the basics of theological education in the Old and New Testaments, church history, liturgy, and theology. Students meet regularly, usually once a week, in seminars under the guidance of trained mentors and are granted Continuing Education Units for each year's work and a certificate at completion of the four years. Similar initiatives of varying depth and complexity continue to be developed and to flourish.

These advances have obviously made inroads. When in 1989 pollster George Gallup prepared a pamphlet entitled "The Spiritual Health of the Episcopal Church" and published by Episcopal Parish Services as preparation for the Episcopal Church's "Decade of Evangelism," his research indicated that a new generation of young adults, aged nineteen to thirty, was poised to respond to a church that actively engaged them in its life and ministry. That new generation has lately emerged in some congregations. Whether fleeing frustrating congregational experiences elsewhere or encountering the church for the first time, this generation seeks a hands-on experience of religion, an integration of spirit and body, of worship and action. When met by clergy and congregations who welcome their gifts and encourage their initiative and engagement, they are taking hold and reinvigorating congregational life.

But all within the church face also the compelling, and competing, complications of our institutional uncertainty. The church is changing rapidly and it is difficult to know just what leadership is needed. For example, in the wake of World War II and the Korean and Vietnam wars, large numbers of men completed seminary and were ordained. But soon thereafter all professions, including ministry, were challenged to admit greater diversity. At the same time, public interest in religion waned; church membership and financial support lagged, so clergy compensation failed to keep pace with other professions. Younger candidates were discouraged by the rigorous demands of ministry while older adults often found affirmation and a second vocation in priestly or diaconal ordination. More recently, an aging church membership awoke to the realization that younger leadership and membership had precipitously declined, and they turned their attention and resources to address this crisis.

Certainly, we are not the first generation of Christians to confront such challenges, nor do I mean to imply that the situation is hopeless. What I do emphasize is that this crisis is largely *institutional* and that the institutional church is a human creation—the organic church, however, is greater than the institution. To use the common biblical image of the church as a body, while there's illness in the body, that illness is largely confined to only a part of the institutional body—and only a small fraction of the institution, being the cadre of ordained leadership and the institutional structures concerned with ordination. Continuing the analogy, an illness in the human body diverts energy and attention to itself, sometimes preoccupying the whole with its pain.

a radical reorientation

Nevertheless, the analogy of the church as the body of Christ presumes a body that is essentially whole and healthy, a body that under normal circumstances enjoys balance. There is far more to the body of God's church than the ordained leadership and the structures pertaining thereto. Indeed, the ordained are now and always have been a means to an end, and not an end in themselves. That end, as stated in the Episcopal Catechism, is "to restore all people to unity with God and each other in Christ." It does this work through the ministry of all its members, lay and ordained, "as it prays and worships, proclaims the Gospel, and promotes justice, peace, and love." Through that ministry, which belongs to all members without distinction, members of the church carry on the "work of reconciliation" in the world.

The church is the last and least arena; the world is the first and primary place of all ministry, a place that is unbounded, simply described as "wherever [we] may be."

The instruments of ministry are similarly broad, extending to "the gifts given [us]." It may be that what is most needed just now, and for the foreseeable future, is a radical reorientation, a turning away from institutional preoccupation and a turning toward the work we have been called and have committed to do in the world, in our lives. That work, for each of us and for all of us, tends to be shaped and expressed in our loves and in our labors.

Q. What is the ministry of the laity?
A. The ministry of lay persons is to represent Christ and his Church; to bear witness to him wherever they may be; and, according to the gifts given them, to carry on Christ's work of reconciliation in the world; and to take their place in the life, worship, and governance of the Church. (BCP 855)

The role and response of vocational discernment in the arenas of each person's loves and each person's labors are sorely neglected and too little evident at the center of congregational life and program. Each and every one of us who is baptized has pledged to give the whole, the fullness, of our life to God. Yet we also believe that we can only know—discern—that fullness in lifelong, living relationship with God and with all that God has made. Knowledge of fullness in any relationship requires time and tools, spaces in our lives devoted to companionship and conversation, skill at asking good questions and practice at listening with ears and intuition.

Each of us stands to gain from a more thoughtful attention to the vocational dimensions and the work of discernment in the making and nurture of human commitments. At present we struggle with conflicted (or nonexistent) theologies of intimate, covenant commitment between two persons. We all need help to make and nurture healthy relationships amid a culture rife with competing messages and images of love, and the messy heap of waste and destruction documented in epidemic divorce.

In the realm of work, more thoughtful engagement of vocational discernment with and among the laity is essential to our stewardship of each person's gifts and abilities. By that I mean that a more intentional discernment goes far beyond mere career planning. Providing encouragement, and lifelong theologically based reflection at every stage of life's journey, and especially in times of significant passage when we must make decisions of major consequence to ourselves and others, offers a deeper sense of the meaning of each person's labor to the life and welfare of the world—and of the moral implications of one's decisions and actions. Intentional conversation and companionship engaging issues of discernment nurtures a healthier self-regard, bringing humility and esteem into balance. And it offers an antidote to the destructive acquisitiveness that equates meaningful living with consumption and competition.

It bears repeating that vocational discernment is the province of every Christian. Limiting discernment to ecclesiastical ordination has led to the assumption that discernment is a discipline only for the professions, for the educated and economic elite. We must embrace the truth that *every baptized Christian is responding to the compelling love of God,* offering his/her life and labor in solidarity with God's work and will for the world. Every believer is called to discipleship, a disciplined life of self-examination and self-giving, a perpetual discerning of vocation that lies at the heart of the church's confessed mission to serve not only its members but all people throughout the world.

Thus the church that professes a commitment to the evangelical mission of restoring everyone to unity with God and each other and a commitment to a lay order whose ministry is "to represent Christ and the church, to bear witness to Christ, and to "carry on Christ's work of reconciliation in the world" (BCP 855) cannot limit vocational discernment to the narrowly particular orders of deacon, priest, and bishop. To advantage ordained vocation by providing it with ample resources for discernment and formation while ignoring the need of every person to equal provision is self-serving. When the church so privileges its professional institutional leadership, it is focused on itself and not the world it is purportedly called to serve and save. It is turned inward, not outward. It is not simply failing at its mission; it has turned its back on that mission, a condition of sin to which the proper first step is repentance, a radical reorientation.

Nor can vocational discernment be limited to lay professionals. The disciplines and philosophies of discernment and vocation are deeply rooted in religion, teaching, medicine, law, and social, political, and civil service, yet even in settings where vocational discernment for the laity has begun, it has seldom reached beyond the professional class. Much is yet to be done to fulfill the gospel's audacious claim that every human life is holy and has equal claim to the promise of fullness.

An extensive survey of American religion reported in 1990 that "the spiritual dimension Americans want includes helping them to find meaning in their lives." It went on to note that "while Americans want spirituality from their churches, they also want practical help. They also want their churches to help them learn how to put their faith into practice; to shed light on the important moral issues of the day; to help them learn how to serve others better and to be better parents. Americans understand that for their faith to be meaningful, it must be real and have a real impact on their day-to-day lives."[3] That desire is hardly limited to one segment of the church or society. If the sales of self-help books and the popularity of media programs purporting to offer advice on every manner of subject are any indication, the yearning for help in practicing faith in meaningful ways is extensive, if not universal.

Finding purposeful direction in service is more than an individual concern; it is applicable to human institutions as well. Just as each individual needs and deserves opportunity and resources to discern how and where one's life best serves God's purposes, so also do "communities" need space and disciplines designed to discern how their collective actions best serve the common good. Among the many challenges facing any Christian community, whether new or established, is determining its purpose, or its particular expression of the larger Christian mission.

All the cultural dynamics that affect our individual lives challenge the church, too. For example, the proliferation of religious options in pluralistic societies, including the multiple and sometimes wildly divergent expressions of Christianity and other religions, fuels a volatile insecurity and a poisonous competition. Among competing claims to truth, who are we to believe and how are we to choose? At its worst, this insecurity is expressed in militant, even toxic, conflict. Many of us have lost arguments and friends to these differences. We are fortunate; for some the loss is greater, even life itself, as numerous wars being waged across religious lines daily remind us. More commonly, in and among American Christians this pluralism drives a frantic scramble for the measurable instruments of power: members and money. Lost in the competitive panic and much of the marketing it engenders are the principles of vocational discernment that have historically directed Christian mission and ministry, overlooked or overshadowed amid the popularity of competing models for church growth.

Thus, alongside the need for individual resources for and attention to individual vocation stands a related need central to the life of believing communities. If, as Christians believe, our individual lives take shape and meaning in a lifelong dialogue with God and God's purposes for all creation, then are not our shared lives and efforts also in dialogue with God and God's purposes? In other words, if God calls individuals, might not God also call institutions into the co-creative enterprise?

Institutions, like individuals, experience aging and maturation, passing through successive stages of growth, including death—a stage Christians believe to be ultimate but not final: in death "life is changed, not ended" (BCP 382). Thus particular congregations and the larger bodies of which they are a part—dioceses, national churches, international communions, and the church catholic itself—are subject to changing circumstances and contexts.

We are neither unique nor alone; every person in every generation is challenged to make sense of life. Meaning and purpose are neither dictated nor imposed, but are revealed in the fullness of life's unfolding. Each relationship with and response to God is intensely and particularly personal. And despite a common mission, each person and every community's engagement with and response to God's invitation to participate in the fullness of the divine life is similarly distinct. Our scriptural heritage and lived traditions have much to contribute to these challenges and our responses to them. We turn to them next.

chapter two

How Did We
Get Here?

It is said that the eighteenth-century Hasidic Rabbi Zusia of Anapoli, before he died, said, "When I face the celestial tribunal I shall not be asked why I was not Abraham, Jacob, or Moses, but why I was not Rabbi Zusia." At the lowest point in my own journey to a priestly vocation Rabbi Zusia's insight would have been very useful. It was the last semester of my last year in seminary. My classmates were excitedly anticipating graduation and interviewing for positions. I was not without cause for anticipation, myself. To all outward appearances I was on a smooth track with a bright future ahead. But appearances were deceiving, literally so. After years of private struggle with sexuality, the truth of who I am was reaching for the light and dragging me reluctantly into reality. I was an emotional wreck, a point driven like a stake into my heart the night I knelt among classmates in a Baltimore church and watched a classmate being ordained. As vested figures crowded round and laid hands upon his head, I distinctly heard an emphatic "No" I knew to be audible and addressed only to me.

In the days that followed I went to my faculty advisor and then to my bishop and I closed the book on the ordination process. I sat in my room late one afternoon amid the profound reality that everything I had most valued and worked for lay in shambles around me. Of one thing, though, I was certain: that the wreck was of my own making. I had steadfastly denied my true self, the self God is constantly creating and calling. It would be years before the pain of that realization would heal and I could fully embrace the wise teaching of Rabbi Zusia.

I learned for the first time that mourning life is not only larger than mourning death, which is only a part of life anyway, but is also a sweeter pain for the heart. It buys one into some small piece of real estate in the common soul. — *Phyllis Tickle*

The details of my own story are less important than the arc of my descent into self-awareness, a plunge I now know to be common to Christian life. Saul, face-down on the road to Damascus, knew the taste of dirt and was not ashamed to include that crucial experience in recounting his own call (Acts 9). But getting from who and what and where we think we ought to be to who and what and where we are created to be often entails a face-down encounter with the dirt from which Genesis says we are made.

Returning to that ancient tale, we discover that vocation itself is literally older than dirt. The biblical account of Creation in the first chapter of Genesis posits a God who calls—literally "says" or "speaks"—a world into being. This creative act of calling precedes the emergence of any being from earth, "being unformed and void, with darkness over the surface of the deep and a wind from God sweeping over the water" (1:2). Despite the insistence of some that the biblical accounts of Creation are to be read as literal and accorded the veracity of empirical science, the text itself seems to resist our certainties. The scriptures are revered as the place where God's divine initiative and human intellect meet. When we engage and explore the Bible, science—from Latin *scientia*, "knowledge"—is challenged by mystery—from Greek *musterion*—which does not mean "beyond knowing," but rather "a hidden truth," a truth or reality yet to be revealed.

That is to say that the scriptures themselves are not simply reference or revelation. They are the very place where God and human beings meet; the scriptures are relational. They are a sacred space within which intimate relationship is lived and expressed. Thus, just as I can claim to "know" an intimate friend or partner, the nature and the excitement of living relationship—relationship with another living being—is always at its core a mystery. The full truth of the other person is always beyond our knowing, and includes all the truth yet to be revealed, all that we meet in the other person moment by moment. That is the source of all delight in relationship, that we are invited to partake in the daily unfolding of each others' lives.

the divine "letting-be"

Bearing this in mind, the story recounted in Genesis 1 offers fascinating insights into vocation. Rooted in the Latin word *vocare*, "to call," vocation in Christian contexts is popularly conceived of as a command, direction, or order initiated by God. A "call" emanating from outside oneself invites, even compels, response. The one called may choose to ignore the call, to accept and confirm the call in obedience, or to resist and refuse the call in rebellion. This common conception of vocation as call and response, or order and obedience, is consonant with operational relationship, the type of relationship associated with hierarchy, located in systems of unequal relationship and authority. This is the kind of relationship we associate with work, with superiors who issue orders and workers who execute them. Indeed, nearly every system by which we have ordered our political, economic, social, and religious life is based and depends upon this inherent inequality.

Operate: from the Latin *operari*, *opus*, "labor, work."

Pronounce: from Latin *pronuntiare*: *pro-*, "forth" + *nuntiare*, "to announce" (from *nuntius*, "messenger")

But the Creation story of Genesis opens otherwise and through this opening invites us into a different possibility. That possibility is rooted in the divine pronouncement itself, the choice of words by which the Creator beckons order out of the chaos in the repeated phrase, "Let there be...." In this divine pronouncement, this "announcing forth," God's creative action is revealed as more artistic than operational.

In this "letting be" there is a respectful distance, a transcendence consistent with a God whose creative impulse seeks not an extension of self, but true otherness—an other, or others, with whom love may be shared, to whom love may be given, and from whom love may be received. God is thus revealed, if only partially. In God's first pronouncement, "Let there be light," mystery is pierced. The God previously hidden in darkness risks the exposure that comes with the light. The first act of creation is an act of self-revelation, as is true also of art. In bringing one's ideas to light, putting paint on canvas, chisel to stone, writing or speaking words aloud, making music—whatever the medium, the artist always exposes something of himself or herself.

Moreover, creation is different from invention. Invention, meaning to chance upon or to discover, suggests accident rather than intent. Invention, which also means to make up or devise, connotes fabrication or manipulation and thus suggests some preexistent material or substance, something less than original. This distinction, central to my reading of the Genesis account, is well stated by the French scholar Didier Maleuvre's assertion that "Art is not inventive, art is creative." He goes on to note that the word "creative" derives from the Latin word *creare*, which is linked to *crescere*, meaning "to grow." A work of art, then, is not something invented, but something that has been allowed to grow. Maleuvre continues:

> To grow means to do the work of being, to let something come forth. Not to engineer, not to presume or anticipate what is going to be, but to let it go forward, not so that it will fulfill a pre-given goal, but really for the sake of letting it grow into being. We can say that a work of art grows for the sake of achieving all that it can be, for the sake of achieving fullness, not for the sake of meeting a preestablished external purpose. So let's say that an artist creates for the sake of letting the work be. We say an artist creates out of generosity, out of the desire to give life, out of dedication to the work. . . . The act of art-making is helping the process, rather than controlling it.[4]

This essential "letting be" is consistent with a God whose own creative activity is purely elective. God is not compelled to create; God *chooses* to create, and in so doing God exercises freedom. In the creative act of "letting be" God not only freely acts, but acts so as to honor the freedom of the creature, freedom being the necessary prerequisite of love. At the very outset of creation, God establishes the terms of relationship: God is free and all that God creates—invites and allows to grow—is free. Without this liberty, true love cannot be. God's creative activity is an expression of God's free, unbounded, and unconditional love. Hence God lavishly, even prodigally, gives that which God desires most to receive—the free, unbounded, and unconditional love of the creation.

As the story unfolds in chapter one of Genesis, elements are announced, proclaimed, and thus endowed with creative freedom: "Let there be light"; "Let there be an expanse [a dome (NRSV)] in the midst of the water, that it may separate the water from water" to become sky; "Let the water below the sky be gathered into one area, that the dry land may appear." Light, water, and earth are invited to be. God does not manipulate water or sky, but instead allows each to be distinct.

Gradually a cooperative spirit emerges from the darkness and chaos of mystery. Creative partnership is literally brought to light. For example, "the water below the sky" is gathered together so that "the dry land may appear." Water is invited to be itself, distinct from sky. When water finds its integrity, its unity with itself ("gathered into one area"), dry land—previously hidden in water's mystery—is revealed. Only when each emerges from darkness into its own does God then name the land Earth and the gathering of waters, Seas.

God then invites earth itself to be creative: "Let the earth sprout vegetation: seed-bearing plants, fruit trees of every kind on earth that bear fruit with the seed in it." The plants and fruits contain within themselves the potential for creative regeneration. Following God's own example, the earth speaks into the mystery of her own newly discovered self and invites into being vegetation and varied living creatures. In subsequent verses God extends a similar invitation to the waters, after which the waters, the earth, and God cooperatively welcome all manner of living thing into being.

But note a distinctive shift of vocabulary. While elements are invited to be—are called—creatures are not the product of God's word. Rather, they are "brought forth" by earth and sea, and then "let be," allowed to grow by God. In this collaborative, cooperative co-creation, world—the earth, sky, sea—and God together make sun, moon, stars, sea creatures, birds, wild beasts, cattle, and, lastly, man and woman. When, in Genesis 1:26, God says, "Let us make man in our image, after our likeness," the collaborative first-person plural suggests a shared activity verified by human science in a creature incorporating the spirit (breath) of God incarnate in bodies made of water and earth.

Produce: from the Latin *producere*,
"to extend, bring forth";
pro-, "forward" + *ducere*, "to lead"

The creatures are "made," "produced"—a particularly felicitous word. Within this cooperative context a whole creation is called forth from dark chaos and each element is "let be," then invited to yield of itself. God's "making" is less mechanical and manipulative (literally "hands-on") than it is a meeting of the other. All that proceeds out of the elemental "letting be" is led forward, is called out—a process often accompanied in the text by naming. Or considered another way, that which proceeds out of the elemental "letting be" is invited into relationship, is met by the Other.

The point I wish to emphasize is that interpretations of the Creation that emphasize a "functional" or "operational" foundation tend toward a theology of human vocation grounded in utility and labor. What I find more compelling, more genuinely "creative," and more consistent with both the highly imaginative and well-crafted story of Genesis 1 is a nuanced reading that honors creation as "letting be." Such a reading in no way diminishes God or God's sovereignty. Neither does it confuse God's transcendence with human notions of superior/inferior, power/weakness. If we Christians learn anything from the Incarnation, it is that God does not seem to want to exercise superiority or power over humanity, does not seek to order us. God's transcendence, and ours, is not a measure of superiority or inferiority. Transcendence is simply otherness, our difference one from the other. God is God. I am human. That is immutable reality. And that is the heart of relationship.

While there is risk in any reading, this interpretation holds a particular peril for security-anxious moderns: So much free exercise suggests a lack of control. This is a particular tension for those whose religious sensibilities cannot or will not tolerate uncertainty and vulnerability. In my preferred reading God and we—indeed, God and all of creation—share the vulnerability. In "letting be" God voluntarily surrenders control, not for lack of love or care, but just the opposite: only by letting all creation freely *be* can love be freely chosen and freely returned.

Moreover, this reading of the Creation story offers a glimpse into the mysteries of theodicy, into the ageless human attempt to comprehend why bad things happen to a world and to people whom God has already pronounced "good." In creation, as offered in Genesis 1, truth is called out of darkness and brought into light. The elements are free to be and it is of their nature to be as they are.

For example, if God can be said to bear any responsibility for the disaster wrought by a massive hurricane, that responsibility lies in God's generous and voluntary invitation allowing the elements "to be." We know that hurricanes are the consequence and confluence of air, sea, and earth, each of which can only be what each is. Yet we also are learning that human intervention or interference can directly affect each of those elements, altering them both in their own right and in relation to one another. The end result, a hurricane, is not so much an expression of divine judgment or nature's fury as it is the logical, natural, and tragic consequence of human impact. It thus falls to all the interrelated parts of such a created order to attend to the being of the other, a responsibility laid bare by any and every human manipulation of the natural order that impedes, supersedes, or contravenes the elements' divine invitation "to be."

The gospel, or "good news," in this interpretation of Genesis 1 is that while it exposes us to risk, this vulnerability is shared with and by God. This is consistent with and evident in the Christian narratives of the crucifixion and in the most orthodox understandings of atonement. In the crucifixion we are particularly met by God at our most vulnerable extreme, joined by God in a death like our own, a death we signify in the act of baptism itself. In this liturgical commitment to relationship in and with the God who lets be—this literal wedding of mutual partners in the vulnerability that lets be—we seal our promise in a watery death. In the waters of baptism "we are buried with Christ in his death."

> We thank you, Father, for the water of Baptism. In it we are buried with Christ in his death. By it we share in his resurrection. Through it we are reborn by the Holy Spirit. *(BCP 306)*

Therefore Christian vocational discernment depends—is grounded in and founded upon—a living relationship with a living God. Within this lively, lifelong dialogue each partner is constantly self-giving and from it proceeds the abundance of life promised to the faithful by Jesus, who reiterates the divine rationale for creation when he declares that he has come so that we "may have life, and have it abundantly," or as rendered in *The New English Bible*, "in all its fullness" (John 10:10). God's love encompasses the whole of creation; all that God pronounces is invited out of darkness and into light, out of the void and chaos into life and being, and called into relationship, each with the other, each and all with God. God's love is indiscriminate. God loves it all, loves us all, without condition. Those who discern, perceive, apprehend, and comprehend the gift of their pronouncement into being and who freely elect to respond to God in love express that response in covenant fidelity in baptism, in commitment to relationship.

The "faithful" then are not defined as such because they maintain "right" belief, or even faultless obedience. Nor are they called "faithful" because they live in fidelity to God as a serf might in fealty obey a lord, or as a soldier is sworn to obey a general. Rather, they are called "faithful" because they have committed to relationship with God. God has pledged to them and they have pledged to God never to abandon the other but to remain in constant communion, each being and becoming to and with the other something new each day. They are called "faithful" not simply because they are functionally loyal to or obedient functionaries of God; they are called "faithful" because they are committed to the *promise* to remain in relationship, to love God.

In Genesis 1 woman and man are of earth's being, earth's bringing forth. Woman and man are "made" or produced—led forward—toward the God who imputes in them God's own image, or likeness. God identifies Godself in them.

Identify: from the Latin *identificare*, "picture oneself": *idem*, "same" + *facere*, "make"

Like other creatures, they are naturally endowed with generative creativity; God does not tell them to "make babies," rather God says to "be fertile and increase" (Genesis 1:28). But (presumably) unlike other creatures,

God identifies in them God's own creative imagination (from the Latin *imago,* "image").

Read this way, Genesis 1 offers a narrative of creation and of human origin that is wonderfully and beautifully symmetrical to the human experience of love: God invites earth to bring forth of itself what it will, and of that "letting be" all manner of creatures are brought forth. Among them God perceives (Latin *percipere,* "seize, understand") and identifies (makes a connection with sameness in) creatures like Godself. Then God *discerns.* God literally separates man and woman—humankind— from the other creatures.

Discern: from the Latin *discernere:*
dis-, "apart" + *cernere,* "to separate"

"Discernment" in classical spirituality entails distinguishing the Spirit of God from other spirits that may be manifesting themselves—such as the spirit of competition or success; the spirit of prosperity or respectability; the spirit of one's family, friends, or colleagues; even the spirit of the times. As one church resource for discernment has described it, "Discernment is a focused endeavor to identify God's Spirit in a situation in order to trace the Spirit's movement and determine where it may be pointing. It is a mode of prayer that builds on a base of knowledge and experience in the ways of God. It can be a profound effort to hear what God is saying."[5]

This description is remarkably like our own maturing and, in the matter of relationships, conveys the need to distinguish between the impulsive and compulsive characteristics that get in the way of healthy relationship. Discerning one's true self means sorting through a tangle of needs, real and imagined, of our own and others' suppositions and expectations, all of which impede intimate partnering. A mature sense of one's own self allows one to discern those who, among the many, are so deeply encountered and understood that they distinguish themselves as soul friends.

Such depth of affection and affinity often eventuates in a literal—and mutual—setting apart in intimate relationship. Some take the form of special friendship, of the type we deem rare and thus set apart from the norm. These are the mentors, the confidants, the companions and guides we hold in highest esteem and deepest trust. In its highest expression such partnering is set apart by vows, by mutual commitment to an exclusivity that separates one relationship from all other relationships in one's life, according that relationship a singular priority. Whether called marriage or otherwise, this ultimate expression of human partnering is rooted in God's special relationship with and commitment to humankind established in creation, reiterated and renewed continually since.

an invitation to co-creativity

The relationship God establishes with humans as conceived in the Genesis narrative is an invitation to co-creativity shared between God and humankind. This activity of co-creation is not simply functional utility. Adam and Eve are not automatons carrying out divine orders. They are neither servants nor slaves to God, or to each other. They are partners with God and with one another. The nature of this sharing relationship is reiterated in the Christian era in the gospels, as when Jesus tells his disciples near the end of his earthly life that he no longer calls them servants, but friends (John 15:15). Paul likewise reminds the Christians in Rome that God's people are not bound in a relationship of fear, like the slave, but rather are beloved and respected as intimate family, as kin.

This latter point may have held (and continues to hold) an even more potent importance for cultures who comprehend in their own lives the clear distinction between a laborious giving of self compelled by a market and its agents, and the literal labor of love, the giving of self as expression of one's partnership in family—family itself being a creature/creation of human love ordered by promise. In other words, God neither compels my love for fear of punishment nor solicits my love with promise of reward; these are the mechanisms and manifestations of power in inequitable systems. An employer compels my loyalty by assuring me of compensation and benefits, and the fear of losing them.

> For all who are led by the Spirit of God are children of God. For you did not receive a spirit of slavery to fall back into fear, but you have received a spirit of adoption. When we cry, "Abba, Father!" it is that very Spirit bearing witness with our spirit that we are children of God. *(Romans 8:14–16)*

The state compels my loyalty by safeguarding my liberty and protecting my safety, and by fear of the courts and law enforcements that can take both away. God invites and encourages my love with a prodigious, even prodigal, promise of unconditional, everlasting love sealed in covenant fidelity.

While it is sadly the case that our relationships are sometimes premised on similar systems of punishment and reward, as we enter the twenty-first century in America, we are questioning such systems. We are more aware and less tolerant of abusive power in the workplace, in civic and private life. Inequality of husband and wife, especially when manifested in physical, mental, or emotional abuse, is no longer tolerated by law and is less and less tolerated by those who witness or experience it. Society in general increasingly deems such abuses dysfunctional at best and criminal in the extreme. Christians in particular increasingly recognize such systems as expressions of sin falling far short of the ideal expressed in the scriptures and exemplified in the narrative of cooperative creation and stewardship.

God grants humans free will not as a particular or special gift, but as a consequence of God's prior, and premier, determination to "let be." Creation fundamentally understood not as divine manipulation but as divine invitation opens fissures in tradition's crust and cracks the walls of human institution. At particular risk are those structures founded upon hierarchy. That is especially apparent in our human role and relationship with the creation.

Genesis 1 presents humankind endowed by God with certain responsibilities in regard to the creatures of the earth that are variously iterated in words like "dominion" and "subdue" (NRSV) or "rule" and "master" (Tanakh) (1:28). These terms are frequently associated with political order and physical power. And that is certainly a legitimate reading. But note the limited scope of that responsibility: the earth itself is not included. Human responsibility is limited to the gifts rendered of earth—gifts of vegetation, of sea and air, of land creatures. Earth is let be.

Stewardship, then, is limited or bounded. Furthermore, our stewardship is subsequent to relationship with God. God articulates divine prerogative; while the elements are "let be," God says "Let us make humankind in our image" (1:26, NRSV). To interpolate, God invites or calls humankind into a particular intimacy, a closeness that allows and includes a sharing of likeness. Or to paraphrase, "I, God, choose to make (pro-duce, "call forward"—to draw near) humankind in such closeness of relationship that they may see me as I am." The logical consequence of such proximity to love is a mutuality between beloveds, each filled with love for the other.

Further, such generous love mutually shared extends to all and everything beloved of each. This abundant mutuality and its product are well expressed in one of the prayers offered for the couple at a wedding: "Give them such fulfillment of their mutual affection that they may reach out in love and concern for others" (BCP 429).

In drawing humankind close, God offers intimacy as evidence of human stature and God's trust, conferring fullness of life upon humans as gifted persons, as partners. This gift—the generous and generative giving of God—is central to and expressive of the fullness of God, the full and complete revealing of God's own being. This is God being God. That God chooses to give is not just characteristic of God, it is the essence of God; it is what makes God who God is.

> The kingdom of heaven is like treasure hidden in a field, which someone found and hid; then in his joy he goes and sells all that he has and buys that field. Again, the kingdom of heaven is like a merchant in search of fine pearls; on finding one pearl of great value, he went and sold all that he had and bought it. *(Matthew 13:44–46)*

This generous, generative giving is also the fullness of God's human partners, who are so intimately bound to God as to be called kin (children) and thus to share this inheritance, being created in God's image. Such generous, generative self-giving is essential, inherent to and in humankind—present in the divine genes, if you will. As such it is, as the parables would have it, beyond purchase, beyond price. It is beyond possession. It is love meeting love, locked in an embrace at once both exclusively intimate and yet expansively, cosmically inclusive.

Therefore, stewardship of creation is neither relegated nor delegated to humankind; stewardship is a collaborative partnership. Any hierarchical or authoritarian reading is antithetical to partnership. While humankind may be designated "first among equals" in creation (all equally beloved of God), the sovereignty—ultimate authority and oversight—belonging to God alone is subservient to a partnership between God and humankind, the closest analog of which is human parenting in its ideal state.

It bears noting that the scriptural narrative records subsequent developments and consequences of this initial relationship. By Genesis 2 it is evident that humankind is not equal to the ideal. God's disappointment is manifest in a destructive flood only slightly tempered by the creatures on the ark being spared. But God's affection, care, respect, and hope for the beloved are not long deterred. As the partnership matures, God's determination to "let be" is tested and tempered. What becomes most apparent is that while God may choose to call humankind forward into intimate relationship, humankind is under no compulsion to receive or reciprocate this gift. Hence God is compelled both by desire (love of the beloved) and design (a determination to let the beloved be) to initiate greater intimacy. Through a series of covenants God draws ever closer, culminating in the incarnation itself, in which initiative God risks ultimate intimacy with humankind.

Dominion: from the Latin *dominio*, "property"; *dominus*, "lord"

For our purposes in this book, this all too brief synopsis must suffice to establish the premise and make the point that vocation is grounded in a relationship of loving mutuality set within a context of "letting be"— respecting each and every partner. In this context the key words dominion/rule, subdue/master prove flexible and expansive. The definitions of dominion or rule are remarkable not for what they allow, but for what they limit. Both dominion and rule ascribe the limit of authority; its definitions are marked in the use of "control," "law," "principle," "code," "territory"—all words connoting boundedness, limitation, and, most importantly, order. They are thus consistent with God's ordering set forth in Genesis 1. This may suggest the image of God as architect or engineer, a creative but disciplined ordering of elements that have their own properties and that are subject to an order consistent with nature. Or it may envision God as cosmic decorator, harmoniously arranging creation in an exercise of divine *feng shui*. But boundedness is also a characteristic of intimate relationship and of commitment. The defining of human boundaries in Genesis 1 is an expression of expansiveness: Humankind is granted, called forward, into a consciousness beyond self, invited by God to share the divine attribute of care, even love, for the produce of earth, the creatures called forth from earth, sky, and sea.

> God blessed them and God said to them, "Be fruitful and increase, fill the earth and master it; and rule the fish of the sea, the birds of the sky, and all the living things that creep on earth." *(Genesis 1:28, Tanakh)*

> God blessed them, and God said to them, "Be fruitful and multiply, and fill the earth and subdue it; and have dominion over the fish of the sea and over the birds of the air and over every living thing that moves upon the earth." *(Genesis 1:28, NRSV)*

"Subdue" is from the Latin *subducere*, "draw from below." "Master" not only means to gain control of but also means to acquire complete knowledge of, as in mastering a skill or discipline. Each expands human dominion or rule to a specific kind of regard, one that enjoins the human to a particular kind of relationship with creation. It is not a relationship of manipulation or domination, much less abuse. Remembering that humankind has been invited and encouraged by God to receive and reflect the image of Godself, it is a relationship that extends to all creatures the same regard that God has demonstrated by "drawing (humankind) from below" *(subducere)* into an intimacy that allows the acquisition of knowledge (mastery). In short, we are invited, allowed, and encouraged to a consciousness and capacity expressed eloquently in the Psalms:

> What are human beings
>   that you are mindful of them,
>   mortals that you care for them?
> Yet you have made them a little lower than God,
>   and crowned them with glory and honor.
>   (Psalm 8:4–5)

With this in mind, our understandings of *vocation* as individual and corporate response to and expression of relationship with the living God move beyond a matter of compulsive obedience to superior order or an acquiescence to preordained determinism. As in any creative partnership, communication is central to the relationship, and it is vital to vocation and discernment. Commitment to mutuality in relationship entails commitment to a conversational imperative, a free, open disclosure of self to the other, without which intimacy cannot be sustained.

Converse: from the Old French *converger*, "to live with"; the Latin *conversari* from *convertere*: *com-*, "together" + *vertere*, "to turn"

This conversational imperative is in lively evidence in the stories and lives of Moses and the prophets, of Jesus and Paul. In theirs and countless stories related in the scriptures, in Hebrew *midrash* and Christian patristic writing, in the witnesses of saints, in sermons and songs ancient and modern we experience this lively, living conversation among partners intimately caught up in and bound to committed relationship.

The inherent risk in conversation is the possibility of change. Again, the stories of Moses and the prophets, of Jesus and Paul, among others, offer evidence that conversation with God can lead us from one way of believing and behaving to another, and that in turn may lead us to a different way of living, one that—as Jesus' own experience and life indicate—can lead us into a trust so radical it lives into death itself.

Yet it is this conversation, this give and take, that is the heart of relationship. The risk involved determines (or should determine) our conversation partners and the quality of our relationships with them. We will not long abide the presence of those we mistrust; if we must share their company, we will guard our thoughts and limit our proximity. Moreover, this conversation is the heart of discipleship. Discipleship is obviously more a matter of education than emulation.

a demanding discipleship

As we have seen, Jesus was at pains to insist that he neither wanted nor had followers, but friends. "I have called you friends," he explains to his disciples, "because I have made known to you everything that I have heard from my Father" (John 15:15). Those who sought to learn from him would not copy his attitudes and behaviors, but would undertake the more difficult business of plumbing their own depths, exploring and embracing their own selves, and shouldering full responsibility for their very being. Or, as he famously expressed it, they would take up their own cross—a cross that was distinct from his.

This learning process, this discipleship, is dynamic and subject to constant variation, consistent with any relationship between and among living beings. Rabbi Zusia's wisdom and my own experience attest that the process of daily, constant learning about self and one's world is a demanding discipleship and the central activity of discernment. Understood this way, we see that any so-called discipleship that obscures or escapes such learning is not worthy of the name; it is just evasion, denial, busyness, and distraction, and ultimately, destructive dishonesty. True discipleship not only dirties the hands, it breaks the heart, opens the mind, and stretches the nerves, as all good learning does. Yet, paradoxically, it is this very dangerous conversation that constitutes the core of discipleship and the intimate heart of relationship with God.

Then Jesus told his disciples, "If any want to become my followers, let them deny themselves and take up their cross and follow me. For those who want to save their life will lose it, and those who lose their life for my sake will find it." *(Matthew 16:24)*

This is true marriage, true partnership. This is the discipleship into which the baptized are invited, and to which they are committed. Like marriage, in this partnership genuine vulnerability and honesty meet love. In that meeting of truth and love we know wholeness, integrity, and their theological synonym, righteousness. Our divine partner, like our earthly mate, assures that our worth is not in utility but in unity, that we are loved and valued not for what we do, but for who we are. We are thus encouraged—literally heartened—to persevere in the exploration of self that leads inevitably to greater wholeness in a process that continues, for the believer, until we attain that state of ultimate union with our partner God and are at last able in that unity to "know as we are known."

For the baptized, all of life and the sum of discipleship is an educational quest, a search for knowledge of oneself. The task of discernment is to glimpse oneself whole, to see and know oneself as God sees and knows us. This knowledge leads to a humility which is neither abasement nor embarrassment, but a right knowledge and sense of oneself as creature of earth (*humus,* "ground") called forth into being, and into relationship. Discipleship and worship are inseparable; both are continuous and simultaneous. The world is a temple and the temple a school, as George Herbert expressed so well in *The Temple* through his poem "The Elixir" (part of which is known to many Christians as a hymn).

> Teach me, my God and King,
> In all things thee to see,
> And what I do in any thing,
> To do it as for thee:

An invocation to vocational discernment, the first verse respects human freedom and transcendence in that it invites God to be revealing, to enter and assist in making meaningful connection between one's life and God's ultimate purposes.

> Not rudely, as a beast,
> To runne into an action;
> But still to make thee prepossest,
> And give it his perfection.

Here Herbert distinguishes human activity and initiative from animal nature. The animal, or beast, driven by instinct, is reactive. The human is otherwise created, endowed with imagination and capable of reflection.

> A man that looks on glasse,
> On it may stay his eye;
> Or if he pleaseth, through it passe,
> And then the heav'n espie.

While a person may see only the shallow reflection of self in a mirror, the divine gift of imagination allows us to see more deeply, glimpsing even in ourselves the bond and the realm we share in relationship with God.

> All may of thee partake:
> Nothing can be so mean,
> Which with his tincture (for thy sake)
> Will not grow bright and clean.

> A servant with this clause
> Makes drudgerie divine:
> Who sweeps a room, as for thy laws,
> Makes that and th' action fine.

In these stanzas four and five Herbert affirms the universality of God's gift of life, love, and partnership to each and every person. No person or contribution is inconsequential.

> This is the famous stone
> That turneth all to gold:
> For that which God doth touch and own
> Cannot for lesse be told.

The final verse reiterates the principle of the first. The poet's intent is not to patronize, to ennoble drudgery for its own sake, but rather to reinforce the principle that if God did indeed speak a world into being and is continually leading all life into fullness, there is then no place where God is not.

Every human undertaking is inherently holy. Even our destructive efforts are part of God's life and bear consequence; because we are committed partners, all that we do bears on one another. This is the weight of sin: that human destruction frustrates God's purposes and God's will for good, even as a partner's failure in any shared project has consequences beyond the one who errs or fails. My failures resonate far beyond my own person and my own welfare. As we now know, even the seemingly innocent act of purchasing food and clothing for our own sustenance can and often does entail grievous wrongs perpetrated in the systems by which we are fed and clothed. It cannot be otherwise in a creation founded upon radical relationship and prodigal partnership.

But the inverse is also true. Because all life begins in God, God has touched it all and, having touched it, renders it all precious, valued, worthy. If the purpose and meaning of each and all human life is active, co-creative partnership with God, the essence of that partnership is the love, trust, and respect inherent in being called "partner." This is a profound mystery: God loves, trusts, and respects us as partners. That God should love us so deeply as to wish to spend all eternity with us. Yet that divine mystery is revealed to the believer as any abiding love is revealed to the lover, in the progressive glimpses granted in simple daily living.

Yes, the dramatic incursion of love is sometimes over-whelmingly present to us. One may experience extraordinary conversion; the apostle Paul told of his own dramatic experience with sufficient frequency and gifts of expression that a written account of it survives in Acts 9. Most of us can recall and recount exceptional experiences of love's potency. But while such experiences may be a touchstone, the cornerstones of relationship are plainer, rougher hewn. Like their architectural counterparts, they are not always readily visible, but are hidden like the frame of a building or, like its foundation, buried in the earth itself. They are more humble and ordinary, the everyday commerce of love between partners that is rightly taken for granted, set aside for the sake of common life. They are, however, no less revelatory.

The cornerstones of relationship are neither obsessive nor possessive, like the egotism of infatuation (and there is a natural egotism in dramatic religious conversion, like its romantic twin). When love matures, egotism gives way to a deep and abiding self-respect grounded in mutuality.

This dynamic giving and receiving is ever present and ever active, yet unobtrusive even to the point of invisibility. Like the conundrum of the chicken and the egg, it becomes nearly impossible to determine which came first, one's love for the partner or vice versa. The Christian participant affirms the primacy of the partner's love: We love because God first loved us. Not because God's love is superior, but because God's being precedes ours. God was here first, and loved us and all creation into being.

The glory of God is a human being
fully alive. — *Irenaeus, Bishop of Lyons*

As the recipient of such life-giving partnership, I am given far more than a body animated by breath. I am given self and a world, purpose and meaning. I am given life in all its fullness. This gift, which is so encompassing it defies easy categorization or naming, is called by Christians simply "gospel," good news. And like all news, it surpasses a single word. It demands a full accounting, a story.

---

evangelism: the stewardship of love

The story of this good news, which like all news stories is highly subjective and shaded by the teller, in Christian nomenclature is called "evangel." The telling of this news is thus called "evangelism" and the tellers, "evangelists." There is a sameness to Christian evangelism—Christian stories of personal experience of love in partnership with God—because Christians come to awareness of this experience through the person of Jesus. Or more accurately, through the stories of those who first apprehended this love in the person of Jesus and whose stories found currency in the lives of others who had not known him but gained access to him and to their own reality in the shared stories. Contemporary Christians seem often to consider evangelism the ultimate mandate, the supreme task of the believer. I am not so persuaded. Neither, apparently, are many of my unchurched contemporaries. Perhaps we as a culture are simply inured by the abundance of so-called news, a barrage of information coming at us from every direction, each claiming its own urgency and importance.

For that reason, I come again to the word "evangel" with a curiosity piqued in the revelation that at the heart of the original Greek root is the word *angelos,* meaning "messenger"—the word from which we derive "angel." An angel is an intermediary, spirit, influence, and manifestation. While speech may accompany mediation, influence, and manifestation, the kind of messenger envisioned is more than a talker. Simply telling the story is not evangelism.

As interesting as the tale of a loving partnership may be, it is neither the richest nor the ultimate product of relationship. The essential "produce" (or "fruit," to use a botanical and biblical term) is fullness of life realized in love, respect, and trust in oneself, in one's partner, and in all shared between them. Thus in exploring the biblical roots of vocation, there remains yet one more consideration, and that is evangelism as the stewardship of love, evangelism as the means and manner of tending the riches of human relationship with a loving God.

Surely one of the most familiar parables attributed to Jesus is the one in which "a man, going on a journey, summoned his slaves and entrusted his property to them; to one he gave five talents, to another two, to another one, to each according to his ability" (Matthew 25:14–30). The one who had received five talents traded with them, and made five more. The one given two talents made two more. But the one who had received one talent dug a hole and hid the money.

When the master returned and settled accounts with them, the one who had received five talents came forward with the original five and the five talent profit, for which he is commended. The one given two talents returns the two along with the two talent increase, and is likewise commended. The one given one talent also came forward, saying, "Master, I knew that you were a harsh man, reaping where you did not sow, and gathering where you did not scatter seed; so I was afraid, and I went and hid your talent in the ground. Here you have what is yours." But the master sees through the self-serving judgment offered as excuse and rationalization. If the master was truly as judged, the very least the servant ought to have done was to entrust the single talent to the bank and return it with interest.

The servant had told a partial truth: he was afraid. Not of the master, but of the responsibility entrusted to him. The servant and his excuses are rejected. In a cruelly ironic reversal of the Creation narrative, the servant and his fear are remanded to their original source, exiled to "the outer darkness." Is the Master being as harsh as the servant judged? Or is the servant's mistrust and fear indication of his free and willful rejection of partnership?

Within each of us is to be found what we might call, as in the Letter of James, "the implanted word" — that is, the dimension of the word that is worked in us by the Holy Spirit and that often takes the form of an unexpected insight or a deep knowing beyond any conscious reasoning. — *Frank Griswold*

This parable is often interpreted as a vocational parable, an allegorical object lesson in the investment of one's God-given gifts, with the coin "talents" being analogous to human skills and abilities. But parables are not allegories. Thus we must be careful of the temptation to the easy or obvious. I suggest an alternative. The "talents"—the real currency God invests in us—is love manifest in gifts of life, freedom, and partnership.

Read in this way, the parable becomes even richer, yielding deeper insight. It is also consistent with Jesus' insistence that proper human response to God's gift is one's whole self, not simply one's skills. The gift I am called to offer is more than what I do; it is the only gift proportional to the fullness of life granted in partnership with God, the whole of my life's fullness.

The commendable stewards in the parable invest everything and are accounted worthy of trust as able partners. The failed steward is fearful and faithless; he is seriously deficient in the requisites of relationship, trusting no one, neither the master nor the bankers, not even himself. He has protected (buried) everything entrusted to him and gives it all back. Truly, the master has lost nothing. Nothing, that is, except the priceless—the partner and the partnership by which all that has been entrusted might grow and bear more fruit.

Total investment of oneself in relationship with God in the world. This is evangelism, the means by which the gospel is mediated. It is in loving as we are loved, in trusting as we are trusted that others come to experience what we have been privileged to share in and with God. How we carry this out in our lives as individuals and as congregations is revealed in careful and courageous discernment, a thoughtful and constant evaluation of ourselves and our partners in the co-creative enterprise we share with God and with all whom God has made. Exploring this continual, life-shaping conversation is the subject and task of the succeeding chapters.

chapter three

God's Gift
to the World

Mike and I met as freshmen in college and by our second year were roommates. We became fraternity brothers; I joined first and soon after became Mike's "big brother" when he pledged. Mike, a cradle Episcopalian, returned the favor in our senior year by becoming my sponsor at confirmation. After graduation, we parted. Mike married his high school sweetheart, whom he had continued to date all through college, and started a career in banking. I entered seminary, was eventually ordained, and began my priestly ministry.

We'd seen little of each other when, after several years, I visited Mike. I found him profoundly unhappy. His marriage was troubled and so was his job. In both the essential arenas of his life, love and work, he was dying. Our conversation that day was not a formal counseling session; I really had no sense that I was present in any capacity except as friend, the cold six-pack we were sharing confirming the intimacy and informality of the occasion. It was one of my first experiences of spiritual direction, which Kenneth Leech insightfully describes as conversation between "soul friends."

> The spiritual director exists to be a friend of the soul, a guide on the way to the City of God. His ministry is one of *diakrisis,* discernment of events, and of *liberation,* enabling individuals and communities to move towards freedom, the freedom of the children of God. He is not a leader but a guide, and he points always beyond himself to the Kingdom and the Glory. Through his love, his silence, his prayer, he seeks to be a light for people in their search.[6]

At some point in our conversation about Mike's dissatisfaction with his work, his aimlessness and confusion, I recall asking, "What do you know how to do?"

"I know how to make bank loans," he replied.

"Well," I offered, "start there and think about what you know how to do best from every angle." As I recall, that's all that was said. We moved on to other matters.

Love and work are the cornerstones of our humanness. — *Sigmund Freud*

It so happened that in the city where Mike lived, an innovative program would soon be tried. The city had over the years taken possession of a large quantity of derelict housing stock. Those houses would be offered to individuals for one dollar each, if the individual could secure the funds necessary to rehab the building, returning it to habitability. Who better to assist those clients than someone who was well acquainted with all the complications of securing a loan from a bank? Mike went to work for a new nonprofit housing initiative where his abilities were put to new use and his perspectives on his work were changed. It was there also that he met the woman who would eventually become his second wife, with whom he parented their lively triplets. Both love and work came into balance in his life.

We remain friends over three decades later. The triplets are in college and Mike, who moved from lending to leadership, seeing the agency through growth and expansion for more than twenty years, has recently retired from the nonprofit and is discerning and pursuing new vocation.

Even through the most ordinary circumstances of our life, Christ the Word manifests his presence. In fact, one might even speak about "the scripture of my own life." Again and again, Christ comes to us clothed in the things that happen to us. — *Frank Griswold*

It would be foolish and presumptuous of me to assume that one casual conversation between friends could so transform a life. I know that there were many more factors in the shaping of his life, but I also know as a friend can know how deeply unhappy he was, and how profoundly happy he became and remains.

This story offers insight into the nature of ministry, both the ministry of one person to another and the profoundly powerful ministry of a life in which love and work find balanced fulfillment. The story is further instructive in that it points to a ministry all the more potent for being unself-conscious. Whatever "service" may have been rendered in this ministry was marked by conversation, an active and loving listening and sharing in which ample space allowed creativity to blossom and from which something new and unexpected could emerge.

By contrast, I recall the story of a visitor to a church who, seeing the building's doors open on a weekday morning, was moved to walk in and look around. There he was met by one of several busy members whose energies were quite evident in well-oiled oak pews, each with prayer books and hymnals oriented in their racks in pleasing symmetry, arrayed in rigid ranks, bounded by spotless merlot-colored carpeted aisles leading in straight lines to a chancel gleaming with polished brass appointments reflecting the jewel tones of bright sunlight filtered through rich stained glass. Before the visitor could say a word, an eager volunteer bounded over and offered, "Isn't it lovely? Can't you just feel God in this place?" To which the visitor ungraciously but insightfully replied, "Hell no, lady. You've got things wrapped up so tight in here, God couldn't get in edgewise!"

Wrapping things so tightly even God cannot get in edgewise is too often evidenced in the complicated processes many dioceses have instituted for discerning ordained vocation. Like those who wisely caution against entrusting national health care to the same folks who manage our other governmental agencies, I am not confident that the diocese is the proper venue for programs aimed at discerning lay vocation. The diocese does, however, have a canonical mandate to "make provision for the affirmation and development of the ministry of all baptized persons." This includes affirmation that all baptized persons are called to ministry. The church is responsible for helping each person identify his/her gifts and discerning where and how best to use them. Entrusting this obligation to local faith communities, the diocese can provide encouragement and ensure accountability by highlighting such efforts in diocesan media, offering education and guidance, and opportunity for recognition by including public affirmation of vocational transition by appropriate liturgical rite and prayer. Why should celebration of new ministry be confined to clergy? Why should commissioning of lay vocations be confined to church school staff, acolytes and choirs?

By valorizing and validating only those ministries that are institutionally self-serving the church has unwittingly contributed to the pain and confusion associated with what is commonly referred to as "the ordination process."

Limiting vocational pastoral counsel and the formation of local discernment to the ordained functions of the church, the more extensive and expansive ministries of the faithful have been shortchanged. If vocational discernment was integral to all congregational lifelong education and ritual, perhaps fewer would seek ordination as the only course of personal validation. And those so called would probably be better integrated both as individuals and as leaders within the complex organization of the church.

Consider the example of a cathedral congregation that begins its program year in early September with a festive day of celebration. At a Eucharist and Commissioning of Ministries, the service booklet lists the twelve Parish Council Commissions, the Wardens and Vestry, and each of their ministries—numbering eighty-two in all. After the Renewal of Baptismal Vows, as each commission is named, participants in the ministries of each are invited to stand and remain standing. By the end of the event I attended in 2006, nearly every person present in a congregation of five hundred was standing and formally commissioned. Afterward a picnic lunch and entertainment filling the lawn outside accompanied an activities fair showcasing the many expressions of ministry and information on how to participate.

discernment throughout our lives

Appreciation of vocational discernment as a lifelong expression of baptism acknowledges the various stages of human maturation as integral to personal vocation. The child's vocation is to be a child; the youth's to be a youth; the student's to be a student, and so on. While this may seem self-evident or simplistic, consider how the application of this principle might radically alter individual and congregational life, and how such alteration stands in opposition to a culture beyond the church that does not widely embrace this principle.

Many of the forces in contemporary culture conspire to accelerate maturation and foreshorten childhood. Even a congregation's impatience or intolerance of children except when they conform to adult standards of behavior is a none-too-subtle rejection of childhood. The gifts of children include their unpredictability, their challenges to established order. Their presence and full inclusion in our lives is as essential to our spiritual growth as it is to theirs.

Childhood is the state in which one fully realizes one's own dependency upon others, one's neediness and vulnerability. — *Joyce Ann Mercer*

"The spiritual quest is integral to the developmental process; it is a common work that generations young and old must share in today's world," writes Sharon Parks. Regarding the "big religious questions" that we all must address she goes on to say:

Young adults are naturally renegotiating questions of their personal future, happiness, God, the ethical dimensions of their choices, suffering, and death. As Andres Nino writes, "These are 'big questions' in the sense that they carry the potential for meaning-making at a profound level, both personally and communally." These are religious questions because they touch the whole of life. [7]

The common segregation of children from parents for all or significant portions of the liturgy and for specialized youth activities or programs may serve the piety and peace of some adults, but it is not serving children and youths. Neither, in the end, is it serving the adults. All are losing. "If you isolate parents from their kids, you are working against the kids," writes youth leader Janie Tinkleberg, who invented the popular WWJD (What Would Jesus

Do) bracelets. "They care about one thing—relationships." Adds Pamela Smith McCall, "They need the affirmation from relationships with parents and other adults. . . . If we want to pass along the Christian faith, then parents must be reflections of that faith and spend time with youth. Youth leaders are saying, Let's step back a little, and make use of what God has given us to help pass along the faith. Let's put parents and the congregational family to work with our youth."[8]

Less than one-half of Protestant teens say church is a very good place to talk about serious issues in their lives. The mainline teens are especially unlikely to say church is a very good place to talk about serious issues. Many Protestant churches do not seem to be giving their teen members the impression that they can safely discuss important life issues in their churches.
— *"Portraits of Protestant Teens"*

Many destructive behaviors and corrosive self-assessments are rooted in inappropriate cultural expectations: the child or youth forced into premature adulthood by too much or too little parental guidance, by manipulative and excessive coercion from adults and aggressive marketers. The middle-aged or senior adult beaten down by inappropriate and unrealistic physical and financial ideals in a culture intoxicated by youth and wealth, where self-worth is based in appearances and acquisitions. These are profoundly vocational issues, central to the truth of who I am, of who and what God invites me to be. The church is called to challenge these and other distortions of human life by offering vocational instruction and icons consistent with the gospel.

This is not an issue of therapy, but of theology. Christians cannot adhere to the summary of the law, which compels a love of God and of neighbor deeply rooted in a right love and appreciation of the God-given self, nor fulfill the mission to restore every person to relationship with God, without attention to this fundamental issue of vocation deeply rooted in and consonant with the divine principle of letting-be. Letting the child be the child, letting the youth be the youth, letting the middle-aged person and the senior be who and what each is made to be is a deeply theological, sacred principle.

While more will be said about congregational vocational discernment in the next chapter, it bears noting here that attention to this principle within each local faith community might radically change a congregation's life and ministry. Do we understand that the heart of our worship as Christians is not the rightness of our rite but rather the wholeness of our lives and our life? The rite is simply the vessel in which we present the offering; the offering is—to quote the eucharistic liturgy—"our selves, our souls and bodies." The holiness of that offering is not made by the context of a churchy rite; the holiness of that offering is made by the content, the wholeness of our very lives.

That wholeness is the product of vocational discernment, evidenced in lives that fulfill God's intention for human being in us, a wholeness offered in and for us Christians in Jesus—the Christ—the One in whom all humankind is both present and redeemed (re-deemed: reaffirmed by God as good, valued, worthy as God did originally deem humankind at creation).

circles of relationships

The story I told of Mike and the potential of conversation to shape a person's vocational discernment indicates how ministry may emerge from friendship. In that instance, the "ministerial moment" was person-to-person, individual counsel shared between friends, culminating in vocational clarity for one of them that led to wholeness in both love and work. The next story begins with two individuals and a request that reveals how the ministry of vocational discernment is manifest like a tossed stone's ripples on a lake's surface, in the concentric circles of relationship in the church, touching a pastor, members and leaders of a congregation, and their bishop. While I could identify key persons or their parish, I have chosen not to only because the experience related has been repeated several times over in different congregations, with different parishes and in different dioceses.

> God is inviting us to go on a journey into his heart and into the good life made available through Jesus.... But entering into this abundant life takes more than wishful thinking. — *www.renovare.org*

Two men, longtime communicants in their parish, visited their parish priest with a request. After living in monogamous fidelity for several years, they wished to affirm their commitment to one another in a more public way, in a ceremony of prayer and celebration consistent with their Christian faith and among the community with whom they shared their lives. Could this be done, they asked.

The pastor was both sympathetic and temperate. Their request was extracanonical and without precedent in that congregation. The priest offered to give their request prayerful consideration and secured their permission to enlarge the conversation, to pursue their request with the bishop and others of the community. The priest conferred with the bishop. There was neither national nor diocesan policy regarding such requests, nor was the bishop inclined to impose his own opinion as policy. Instead, the bishop counseled the priest to take the request to the parish.

The priest conferred with the parish vestry. Together they concurred that a small congregational committee would be invited to meet with the couple, to continue the conversation about their request—to discern a way forward. After meeting a number of times with the couple, the committee sat with the vestry and expressed satisfaction that the couple's request and their lives as evidenced in their congregational participation and community life was consistent with their understanding of covenant love as expressed in Christian marriage, excepting only the gender of the partners. The committee saw no impediment to supporting the couple's intention to live in faithful commitment.

The vestry decided that given the lack of precedent, the couple's request to have their ceremony within the church deserved congregational conversation. In a short and irenic congregational meeting the parish granted consent. The commitment service was undertaken with solemnity and festivity, celebrated by the couple and their Christian congregational family.

The story offers several learnings suggesting broader application. When I first heard of such an incident, I was struck by the wisdom and humility of all involved. The couple making their request made no demand nor expressed any expectation. The priest assumed no authority to grant or deny the request. The bishop deferred to parochial counsel and conversation. The vestry delegated responsibility to a wider body of lay members in committee. The vestry and committee sought the counsel of the congregation. In sum, the whole body shared the burden of the pastoral request. And the whole body shared the responsibility and the joy of witnessing the commitment of two of its members to a faithful, loving life.

None involved in this story treated the gay couple's request as a problem to be solved. Rather, it was an invitation to discernment. In the series of conversations required to reach clarity, those involved were granted a rare opportunity to encounter and engage many layers of learning about what it means to be Christian. Considering the wider networks of relationship beyond those personally involved—all the friends and family who learned about and discussed the various aspects of this process with those at the center—this story exemplifies Christian witness. Any privileged to see the respect and trust manifest throughout were granted a powerful icon of faith, a literal window into human relationship grounded in and with God.

Why is a similar process not used when any couple seeks to undertake the marriage covenant in community? Why is premarital counseling normally relegated to private consultation with the parish priest and, occasionally, a professional or process designed to assess compatibilities? The design that emerged from the gay couple's request of their parish was similar to the canonical process which aspirants seeking affirmation of a call to ordained ministry are required to undertake.

Quakers know this practice as a "clearness committee," convened at the request of any member seeking guidance in a time of decision or transition. A few Episcopal congregations now offer similar opportunity. Surely, if the church offers and expects so enlarged a conversation and shared responsibility in the ordering of episcopal, presbyteral, and diaconal vocations and covenants, it might offer and expect as much of those seeking affirmation of a call to marriage, family, and covenant commitments of similar importance to the welfare and life of the community.

---

discernment in institutions

The next stop on this anecdotal journey is something of a shrine to many a modern church leader: Willow Creek Community Church in South Barrington, Illinois. Often

cited as a leading example of successful church development and growth in America, this church is much studied
by those seeking to emulate its achievements. Without
endorsing or denying this church's ministry, I wish to
suggest nevertheless that those who study this congregation would do well to consult its history carefully and
thoughtfully. The most valuable lessons to be learned are
less evident in the charts and graphs and program details
than in the simple recounting of its genesis.

In 1991 a Harvard Business School student prepared a
now-famous case study of Willow Creek Community
Church, at the outset quoting Willow Creek's senior
pastor, Bill Hybels: "It was never our intention to build a
big church. From the very start, our vision was to just 'be'
the church that God intended us to be."[9] It would be
difficult to find a more apt description of congregational
vocation.

The story of Willow Creek is dominated by the eventual numerical and financial success of this church. Yet
behind the near mythic story of corporate success lies one
person's spiritual and vocational biography. The "back
story" begins with the personal vocational discernment of
Bill Hybels himself. As the tale is told in the Harvard case
study, Bill's discernment is rooted in a rich mentoring
relationship with his own father, who seems to have taken
quite thoughtfully his vocation as parent. Driving home
from church, his father one day mentioned a friend at
work named Bob, whose wife had been diagnosed with a
terminal illness. Bob was asking Bill's father about God
and Bill's father wondered aloud if he should invite Bob to
church. The thirteen-year-old Bill hastily blurted, "Oh
no, Dad! Whatever you do, don't do that!"

"Even as a child," says the case study, "Bill sensed that
somehow church wasn't very inviting to the nonbeliever."
While the anecdote reveals Bill Hybels as a young church-
goer with a keen appreciation of how off-putting tradi-

tional churches can be, ironically, to those they are called to serve—which is to say, everyone outside the church—there is more than that evident. The trust evidenced between father and son reveals a rare appreciation of and respect each for the other. The father trusts that his thirteen-year-old son might help with a personal, and very adult, dilemma. The son trusts his father enough to tell the unvarnished truth without fear of dismissal or worse.

This mentoring served Hybels well when, as a young adult, he was asked to lead a small youth group. In the course of that experience, his leadership is remarkable for its conversational mentoring. "After leading this group for some time he asked members if they wanted their friends to become Christians. They all enthusiastically replied, 'Yes!' Bill told them to pray for their friends and invite them to the Bible study. He was taken aback by their response: a wall of blank glassy-eyed stares." Hybels asked the simple question, what's the matter? Then he listened as the youths offered thoughtful criticism. Their shabby basement meeting space was an embarrassment; the music was, too. Hour-long education sessions were too long, and Bible study unmoored from life issues was a nonstarter, especially for seekers.

What followed is remarkable in every sense. Perhaps most remarkable is that the pastor, the leader, actually listened, respected, and honored what his colleagues in ministry—the youth—had to say. Responding to the collective conversation, his ministry was genuinely "of service" and the group swelled in two years from twenty-five to over one thousand. More to the point, Hybels learned (discerned) four philosophical principles that continue to shape and guide his and his congregation's ministry:

+ Every believer has the responsibility of being a witness in one's faith and relationship with God.

+ The needs of the seeker differ from those of the believer.

+ Believers must respect the individual's process of a faith decision and the journey one must travel to maturity in their relationship with God.

+ Every believer is a minister, gifted by God for the benefit of all in the church.[10]

Note the prominence of relationship with God and respect for individual responsibility and agency in that relationship. Note, too, the fundamental respect for the ministry of every believer. Because Willow Creek ministries proceed from personal initiative and leadership instead of need, "space" is therefore granted to creativity, and a greater likelihood that new and thoughtful ministries will emerge from the diverse gifts of the membership. While hardly perfect, the principle to note is the contrarian, but theologically consistent, wisdom that the institution (Willow Creek Community Church) serves its members in their ministries of service in and to a larger community. Yes, Willow Creek Community Church is equally served, as evidenced in their impressive resources so obviously and abundantly funded by the membership. But one can argue that this congregation represents a very large and complex example of coopera-tive, collegial, creative ministry. The originating principles identified by Bill Hybels and adhered to in his own personal vocational discernment, as well as his leadership in congregational discernment, suggest a thoughtful and fruitful trajectory for ministry.

These stories of individual vocation and discernment center largely on a demographic common to books like this one. Nearly all mentioned thus far are privileged by education and experience, as are most ordained clergy and their lay colleagues in church leadership. Many mainline Protestant churches, and notably the Episcopal Church, have grown comfortably accustomed to a life dominated by such people. Yet churches have always numbered among their membership those who have little or no education, few financial resources or employment opportunities. With rare and laudable exception, congregations and their leadership have tended to treat even the most beloved of these members more as a custodial or charitable responsibility than as full partners and colleagues in ministry.

Considerations of vocation and discernment have tended to center on those who are privileged to have work and secure intimate relationships, or the prospects of them. But the reality is that growing numbers of Christians, even in the mainline churches, are poor. And the majority of the world's population is overwhelmingly poor. So what do vocation and discernment have to do with them?

Recovering a theology of Christian vocation that posits each person's vocational worth not in utility but in his/her origin in God, a theology rooted in divine "letting-be," offers specific opportunity for the church to oppose the prevailing North American culture and those theologies it has spawned that equate spiritual and vocational fulfillment with financial success, social status, and political power.[11] This may be one of the most important countercultural witnesses of the Christian church in the developed world, the very world which has embraced economic models as the frame of all meaning and worth and daily exports those models to the ends of the earth.

The principal theological activity of every human being is to comprehend what life means—not just in general, but very much in the particular. What does my life mean? What does it mean that I was born as I was, when I was, where I was? What does it mean that I have some abilities and not others? Some opportunities and not others? What choices shall I make and how might those choices bear upon my life's meaning?

The vocational impulse seems from the literal beginning to have been about these questions. This engagement and its record is collective, a collaboration of which an early written example is the biblical narrative of Genesis. For the authors of that narrative and for us, their heirs, the fundamental meaning of human life begins in God, a single Creator who has rendered a whole (unified) creation. God has chosen us, chosen you and me. The meaning of our lives, my life, is a wholeness grounded first and foremost in unity with that God. A whole life lived with integrity in a truth embracing the fullness of myself, a whole life lived within the fullness of the truth of God and the world issuing from and embodying that truth.

The work of the church for centuries to come, as for centuries past, is to accompany—to be a company of pilgrims, travelers on a journey, on a road important not so much for destination as for direction, one direction leading to unity, integrity, God; the opposing direction tending toward chaos, disintegration, disunity. Hence the Christian emphasis upon orientation. A community that characterizes sin as straying, missing the mark, as lost sheep, and defines the antidote to that sin as *metanoia,* repentance—a literal about-face, a change of direction that reorients, that turns us around and sends us back on the path to be reconciled, to make peace with ourselves, with our neighbor as the way back to unity with God. A community that understands life as journey, as meaning making, not meaning made, fixed and found. A community committed to life on the road, with all the challenges and vicissitudes of travel.

If vocation is the essence of one's being, ministry is the incarnation of one's vocation, the physical shape and manifest expression of vocation, the incarnation of one's unique life in relationship to the whole of creation. The very root of "ministry" (Latin *ministerium,* "servant") is service, and service assumes relationship. Service always presumes an object, or other, even when the one being served is oneself.

All mankind is of one author, and is one volume; when one man dies, one chapter is not torn out of the book, but translated into a better language; and every chapter must be so translated.... No man is an island, entire of itself.... Any man's death diminishes me, because I am involved in mankind; and therefore never send to know for whom the bell tolls; it tolls for thee.
— *John Donne, Meditation XVII*

Because we ascribe the whole of creation to a single source, as we Christians attest in our creeds, we deem our very presence in the world as gift. Each life is given, not only to the self but to the whole of creation of which that self is but a single member. Even the person who "does nothing" is still a valued gift and substantial contributor as part of creation's own essential ecology. This principle is amply articulated in Christian scripture and literature:

> Look at the birds of the air; they neither sow nor reap nor gather into barns, and yet your heavenly Father feeds them.... And why do you worry about clothing? Consider the lilies of the field, how they grow; they neither toil nor spin, yet I tell you, even Solomon in all his glory was not clothed like one of these. (Matthew 6:26–29)

The confusion of giftedness with talent or utility is not only spiritually corrosive, it is specifically non-Christian. Each person's worth abides in his/her being a creature—a creation—of God. In the most profound sense each of us truly is God's gift to the world. This sense of relatedness and the self-worth that it encourages lies at the heart of the Christian perception of reality. The singular mission of the church, as articulated in the Catechism of the Book of

Common Prayer, is "to restore all people to unity with God and each other in Christ" (BCP 855). This mission assumes God's love of and unity with us. The mission is to restore relationship; it aims at affirming and ensuring this relationship as the fundamental prerequisite to Christian faith, life, and worship.

Worship: from the Old English *weorscipe,*
"worthiness, acknowledgment of worth"

Indeed, the very meaning of worship is predicated upon this sense of self-worth, the affirmation that oneself, one's life in soul and body, is an offering fit to be placed before God. We are worthy because of our origin in God's own creative will. Not for what we do, but for what we are.

Ignoring this worth, or refusing to accept, affirm, and honor it in ourselves, not only impoverishes us, but because of our radical connectedness to the whole creation and our part in the ecology of the whole, robs the world of the gift God intends us to be. Whatever the basis of this estrangement, the consequence is defined as sin—sin not merely as wrongdoing, but as a radical disconnectedness from primary relationship with God. Disconnection of self from self, of self from neighbor, and as we are increasingly aware, of self from the whole of creation. As psychologist Mihaly Csikszentmihalyi (pronounced *Me-high Chick-sent-me-high*) has noted, "We now realize that our unique heritage—the reflective consciousness that lulled us into believing for a while that we were forever destined to be the crown of creation—brings with it an awesome responsibility. We realize that being at the cutting edge of evolution on this planet means we can either direct our life energy toward achieving growth and harmony or waste the potentials we have inherited, adding to the sway of chaos and destruction."[12]

For the Christian, ministry is not merely what one *does,* a set of behaviors or skills. Ministry is the substance of one's whole life, the living of one's life in relationship with and in service to God, neighbor, and self. As such, it is ultimate giving, as essential to one's being human as pure giving is the essence of the God in whom our lives have their origin, the God whose image we bear. Any breach or interruption in this dynamic relationship of gifts and givers is a legitimate concern of the church. For the gift of God is transmitted in relationship. Indeed, the gift *is* relationship. Such self-giving is the very essence of God. As one theologian characterizes the incarnation, "When God becomes human, we are being brought to God.... God is doing what God is always doing, attempting to give all that God is to what is not God."[13] Introducing and, when appropriate, restoring each person to this fullness of incarnate human being is the mission, the *raison d'être*, of the church.

Given the myriad talents, skills, gifts, and passions of the diverse collective of the baptized, the scope of ministry is nearly limitless. Yet most definitions of ministry are crabbed and cramped, limited to the relatively small body of Christians represented in the orders of bishop, priest, and deacon. Moreover, an appreciation of the worth of each person as a valued, contributing component in the ecology of creation suggests that just as there is no place where God is not, there is no place where ministry is not practiced. The integrity of God's creative activity, and the creation that proceeds from it, demands this wholeness. Anything less is less than holy, for true holiness is predicated upon this radical integrity, this essential, ecological wholeness.

transforming lay ministry

Still, "lay ministry," with scant exception, is most often conceived as an extension of the work of the institutional church. Assistants in the liturgy. Lay visitors to the sick and shut-in. Lay workers with responsibility for special-ized work like parish administration, education, youth, or music. With considerable fanfare and self-congratulation, churches offer training, licensing, and opportunity for "lay ministry" with no apparent awareness that limiting lay ministry to institutional tasks is selfish and self-serving. It is as though lay ministry has no validity beyond the bounded walls of "church."

> The Bible is full of God's call to all human persons but we have so often narrowed the idea of vocation to mean merely a call to religious orders. Now is the time to recover a sense of the call of God in each one of us . . . to be watchful, to be expectant and to look for His always surprising Advent in this new wired-up world rather than in a continuation of the same old trends. — *Richard J. Chartres, Bishop of London*

Similarly, under the somewhat misleading name "total ministry," a number of Episcopal dioceses have instituted extensive programs to perpetuate struggling congrega-tions. Under these programs the laity are trained and authorized to carry out the functions normally under-taken by an ordained priest. While these and similar initiatives in other denominations represent institutional innovation, their ends are aimed at perpetuating congre-gational life and routines. Though these efforts expand the roles of congregational leadership and mission, they are not the same as assisting the laity in discerning and living their distinct vocations in service to the world.

When "enabling the ministry of the laity" means insti-tutional control over lay energies, deploying lay gifts in service to institutional ends, furthering the work of the institutional church with volunteer and low-wage workers, then the true "enabling" in such initiatives is the perpetuation of this institutional captivity. Lay ministry is not the corralling of lay energies for the service of the institutional church. Lay ministry is the living expression of every baptized person's vocation in daily life. Just as Moliere's comic character in *Le Bourgeois Gentilhomme (The Would-be Gentleman)* was surprised to learn that he'd been speaking prose nearly his whole life without knowing it, so most Christians might well be surprised to learn that their whole life has been and is a ministry.

Proceeding from this principle, the church's ministry, or servanthood, is (or ought to be) at least in substantial part to serve the laity in each person's discernment and implementation of vocation. In this chapter I have offered several anecdotal suggestions of what this servanthood looks like. These are not intended as models; models too frequently morph into templates to be imposed on any and every person or situation, imposing expectations when what is to be encouraged is a creative and sensitive engagement with each person. When the model actually works, it may still become idol.

The Christian creeds affirm that all creation originates in God, but there remains the creativity of collaboration, the uniting of elements into new relationships that invite new being, new creation. Bringing disparate elements of creation together is a mediating ministry. Distances, estrangements, are overcome and new harmonies issue in new creation. The writer changes the relationships of words. The composer alters the relationships of notes; the orchestrator introduces new instrumental relationships. The visual artist alters space, color, light, media. Inventors rearrange the relationships of varied components. In each endeavor something new emerges and, frequently, properties inherent in something—or someone—long known are discovered, brought to the light of day and new consciousness. And occasionally the historian discovers that the discovery itself is but a recovery, the restoration of some reality once known, long obscured. The co-creative partnership we share with God and with our neighbors thus encourages genuine conversation with one another, and requires that we listen and accompany with care.

In fact, accompaniment is an apt metaphor for the collaborative service that is Christian ministry. The musical accompanist is essential to the whole experience of the music. But the accompanist seldom takes the lead and the good accompanist never overpowers the other musicians. To be an accomplished accompanist is to be intimately engaged in a musical conversation, an ensemble of "voices" who are each listening with care to the other and sensitively offering his/her part with impeccable timing and intonation. In the end, the first-person "I" becomes partner in a collaborative mission, is incorporated into the cooperative "we." A ministry of accompaniment appreciates that the essential "letting-be" of creation is evidenced in a mutual, even universal, respect for the worth of every person, of everything God has created.

The counterintuitive but commanding wisdom of many a growing Christian congregation indicates that those congregations that expect more of their members tend to grow both in number and depth. But much depends on just what that "more" is. More programs for programs' sake? More worship for worship's sake? Probably not, though vibrant congregations often offer many varied programs and rich worship. But they also offer members more responsibility for engagement with the very real and substantive matters of human being, individually and in community. Programs, activities, and worship tend to emerge from lay initiative and flourish with encouragement and assistance from parish staff and congregational leadership. Freed from staff control and its limitations, congregational life expands, energizes, enriches, and elates; that such opportunities and experiences also educate and equip the faithful to fulfill their own lives is no small coincidence.

Leadership in congregations noted for their vitality, depth, and richness most often takes the form of mentoring. Mentoring is distinguished by a mutual trust—not just the trust of the advisee for advisor, but the trust of the advisor for the advisee. This kind of teaching, which is apparent in the relationship Jesus cultivated with and among his disciples, has only lately emerged from a long obscurity. Mentoring was a central practice of Jesus that has long defined and distinguished Christian life, not because it "works," but because it is genuinely holy—truly whole. It is a way of being in the world that has integrity with the life and gospel of Jesus. It is not just "a" way, it is *the* way that followers of Jesus relate to one another and to the world.

A friend is someone we know and respect, someone whose very difference we treasure and whose gifts we nurture. A friend is not a competitor, but someone we hold in mutual regard and affection. — *Kevin Thew Forrester*

Why is this important to the church in the twenty-first century? Because it has been true of and important to the church in every century. Moreover, lack of integrity is a widely documented criticism of the modern church. Not just the obvious and sometimes criminal violations of trust like sex abuse and financial shenanigans, but the general disjuncture between the principles espoused by the gospel and the ways those principles are practiced (or not) and perceived, especially by those marginal to or outside the church. Restoring integrity means changing the way church leadership relates to membership, and changing the way both relate to those outside the church, practicing a radical trust that does not come easily.

The God who *lets be* invites the creature to co-creativity, to share responsibility for life, for his/her life, for the life of the world. Vocation and discernment are not limited to what one does in the utilitarian sense; we are not just what we "do," nor is the value or meaning of one's life limited to quantifiable achievement. Vocational discernment does not consist solely in matching aptitude to opportunity, finding the "right" job or the "perfect" mate. For example, retail management was never my idea of the right or perfect work for me, but when offered, I chose it. The meaning of that decision later emerged with greater clarity, as the experience and learning derived from that work proved essential to the demands of a succession of later ministries. At the outset of each new venture, however, what I most needed was encouragement— courage to choose, to decide.

> Decide: from the Latin *decidere:*
> *de-* "off" + *caedere,* "cut"

Deciding entails risk. To decide means to cut away, to commit to one among multiple options. The fear of making a wrong choice, of failure, is at heart a fear of rejection, of being literally cut off. My decisions to defer ordination and to take a position in retail management were both accompanied by a fear that each decision might be met with rejection by friends and loved ones, might be my own rejection of God.

Vocation and discernment are fundamentally about decision-making and meaning-making; vocational discernment in Christian community is about accompanying one another in this lifelong process, church as a space of radical trust. Equipping, yes, but encouraging, too. Giving one another heart—courage—to accept the truth of oneself, of the world, of God. Giving one another the courage to choose, to decide among a competing array of options. Giving one another companionship in the discernment and embracing of the meaning of those choices, and out of that meaning-making, to choose again.

Freeing vocation and discernment from utilitarian, economic bindings allows us to see more clearly how to accompany any person and all God's people, to render a ministry of genuine Christian service to each and all. The person whose array of choice is circumstantially constrained—the child, the senile elder, the homeless person, the addict, the prisoner—nonetheless makes choices, and each life has meaning. Eleanor is a lay spiritual director and member of a lively urban congregation. Living with multiple sclerosis and assisted by a motorized scooter, she found a new vocation at midlife when illness imposed change in her routine and career. A volunteer hospital chaplaincy opportunity prompted her to undertake a certification program in "The Art of Pastoral Care." She then spent five years as a special student in a nearby non-degree seminary program that included many of the foundational courses for professional lay and ordained ministries. Concurrently, she also completed a two-year program in spiritual guidance.

"Before entering seminary," she writes, "I'd inquired about and found a spiritual director who was extremely helpful in sorting out all that was happening in my life. I turned 55 and decided to sell my house and move into a condominium. Dad died after a three-year struggle with prostate cancer. My three children were married, had their own homes, and were settled in significant careers. I already had two grandchildren but a third and fourth were born while I was at seminary. Throughout [these five years] I continued to serve as a volunteer hospital chaplain. While at seminary I discerned two important things, my call to spiritual direction and the reason I'd struggled with the Episcopal parish into which I'd been born."

In 1998 she moved from her conservative birth parish to a diverse downtown parish with a breakfast program for the poor and homeless members of the community. Today she returns regularly to the seminary to provide spiritual direction to individual students. And in turn with others at her parish she leads a 7 a.m. Bible study especially welcoming the homeless members of the community, and attends an 8 a.m. Eucharist followed by breakfast. The Bible study is variable; one season "Gospel Art" filled the hour. She came to this ministry when a former rector charged four parishioners, a seminarian, and a staff person, Eleanor among them, with bringing the concept of discernment to their parish.

> The Church is first of all a kind of space cleared by God through Jesus in which people may become what God made them to be (God's sons and daughters), and that what we have to do about the Church is not first to organise it as a society but to inhabit it as a climate or a landscape. It is a place where we can see properly—God, God's creation, ourselves. It is a place or dimension in the universe that is in some way growing towards being the universe itself in restored relation to God. — *Rowan Williams*

They met for nearly a year, and after spending time in study and prayer they decided to start with group spiritual direction as a way of introducing an aspect of discernment. "We continue to have two spiritual direction groups that meet on a monthly basis," Eleanor explains. "We used the Quaker Clearness Committee model when two parishioners wanted to start an environmental ministry. They did so and it's been a wonderful way of reminding us all of our responsibility to the environment. We have a rooftop garden that produces vegetables! We've also used the Clearness Committee model for our vestry candidates, asking each of them to express themselves on three points: their desire to serve on vestry; the gifts they will bring to the vestry; and their awareness of God's call. Hopefully, in time all committees and most especially the vestry will practice discernment in their meetings. And also, as parishioners get used to the concept, they will come to the discernment group when faced with a dilemma or are at a crossroads in their lives."[14]

In *Pastoral Care,* Gregory the Great offers a beautiful image of pastoral ministry: "Those who carry the vessels of the Lord are those who undertake, in a reliance on their way of living, to draw the souls of their neighbors to the everlasting holy places."
— *Gregory Jones*

How we accompany each other in the process of meaning-making and decision-making may vary, as the following story from a widely circulated essay by John McKnight relates:

I met a remarkable woman in a little town in southern Georgia. She worked for a service agency responsible for mentally retarded people in a three-county area. Her agency decided it was too focused on deficiencies and needed to think about the gifts, contributions, and capacities of the people who were its charges. So this woman began spending time with the people the agency had once called "clients" to see if she could understand—in their homes—what gifts they had to offer. She went to the home of a forty-two-year-old man who had been the victim of special education—segregated education. His name is Joe. He has one short leg (at least he limps), and he doesn't speak the way a lot of people speak. (I'm not sure what label deficiency-finding psychologists would give him. But I'm sure they would give him one.)

At age twenty-one, Joe had no place in society. So he went home to a pig farm. Every day he did two things. He fed the pigs twice a day, and he sat in the living room where he listened to the radio. (He couldn't see to watch television.) The woman told me that after four days at Joe's house she couldn't find his gift. "But on the fifth day," she said, "I realized what his gift was: He listens to the radio."

"I found out that three people in town spend all their time listening to the radio, and they get paid for it. One is in the sheriff's office, one in the police department, and one in the local civil-defense office. So I looked at each of these places where a person sits, listening to a radio all day. I liked the civil-defense office best. It's a voluntary organization. They have a house that somebody gave them; so the voluntary ambulance people sleep in its bedrooms. There's a desk and sitting right by the desk is a radio getting all the calls from the county. At the desk sits a twenty-seven-year-old woman who listens for calls and dispatches volunteers when someone needs an ambulance."

So she told the dispatcher, "I have somebody here who likes to listen to the radio as much as you do. I'd like to introduce you to him." And so she introduced Joe to her, and they put a chair on the other side of the desk, and he sat there every day listening to the radio.

This little house is also the neighborhood community center. Somebody is always there. People come and talk and drink coffee in the dining room. Sometimes they show movies. Whenever anybody was there, Joe would go in. Everybody came to know Joe, and he became a part of that neighborhood. When Christmas came, the volunteers gave Joe a radio of his own to listen to at home in the evening because Joe had been with them and had shared his gifts in the face of their hospitality.

Joe began to go downtown at noon to eat at the diner. One day he went into the diner and the owner of the diner said, "Hey, Joe, what's happening?" Joe looked at him and said, "The Smith house over in Boonesville burned down this morning. And out on Route 90, at that turnoff where you can have picnics, there was a drug bust. And Mr. Schiller over in Athens had a heart attack." Everybody in the diner stopped talking and looked around at Joe. They couldn't believe it. They realized that Joe knew the answer to the question "What's happening?" because he listened to the radio all morning.

When I went to visit this town and the woman who introduced Joe's gift of listening to the radio to the community, I saw an incredible thing. I saw, first of all, that the dispatcher and Joe were in love with each other. Then when I went with Joe to lunch, I saw that everybody who came into the diner came over to Joe first and asked, "Joe, what's happening?" And I realized that I was in the only town in the United States that now has the gift of a town crier.

The woman told me she was planning to take Joe over to the newspaper editor. It had occurred to her that in this little town with a little newspaper and one editor, the editor couldn't possibly know "what's happening." But by noon Joe knew. And if Joe would go over and talk to the editor every noon, the grasp, the breadth, the knowledge of the newspaper and what it could report would expand mightily.

So Joe is now a stringer for the local *Gazette*. He showers his gifts on the community because somebody knew that community is about capacities, contributions, and hospitalities—not about deficiencies, needs, and services.[15]

Hospitable support for individuals in their vocational discernment, whether offered by individual mentors or by mentoring communities, is the historic ministry of the church. In this chapter we have considered how individual and corporate acts of mentoring ministry may serve this individual quest. Next, we turn to vocational discernment in the community of the congregation.

chapter four

Why Are
We Here?

Vocation and discernment are words easily and frequently associated with the personal search for life's fulfillment in meaningful work and relationships. Less commonly encountered is the possibility that the disciplines of discernment and the language of vocation hold considerable potential for larger, broader applications, that vocation and discernment are also the province of congregations and other human communities.

Most of us are familiar with the "mission statement," a now ubiquitous essential whenever two or three are gathered together with intent to accomplish anything. There are often similarities between a group's vocation and its mission statement. But just as there is far more to one's vocation than the statement of intent, so there is often far more to a congregation's vocation than its mission statement. Indeed, as my own story of vocational vicissitude in the previous chapter suggests, even the best laid intentions can and do go astray, get radically altered and are sometimes dashed altogether. We do not always know where our path is leading, nor do we need to know; this is the nature of a life of faith. Therefore, rather as I must hold fast to my faith in God, but sit loose in the saddle of life, so the Christian congregation balances steadfast faith with a perpetual readiness to respond to what relationship with God might demand in any given moment or circumstance.

Psychologist Mihaly Csikszentmihalyi uses the term "flow" to describe this state of readiness, the integration we experience when all aspects of life are functioning at maximum capacity and efficiency, when one is fully engaged, fully focused, and fully available to the moment. What he describes as "flow" is the balance of skill, challenge, and commitment. This experience, this "flow," is not limited to any particular endeavor. Artists seem adept at describing the experience, as when the musician professes to have been so focused in performance as to be one with the music, a condition that assumes also a oneness with the instrument and the audience. But this wholeness can be experienced in any instance of one's life. The devoted agriculturist or gardener, the cook, mechanic, or laborer may be similarly focused. Nor is the experience of flow confined only to the arena of work. The wordless communion of relationship and the profound experience of sexual union are but two of the more prominent places where we may experience flow in love.

But how is this flow manifest within a community's life and vocation? How do we experience this coherence in our collective life? There are many possible answers to those questions, but in recent years American churches have tended toward materialistic answers; numerical and financial increase have come to define and quantify capacity and efficiency. For some congregations, especially those independent churches not tethered to (or encumbered by) denominational structures, this route represents a certain prudence and pragmatism; someone, after all, has to pay the bills.

In congregational life, as in our personal lives, following the right course entails risk. Having studied and profiled the "best practices" of numerous congregations, Paul Wilkes writes, "Excellent churches have unconsciously adopted a certain... approach where convention or convenience does not rule, but effectiveness or the potential for effectiveness does. Who are we and what are we trying to do? This is not about denominational standards, but a higher standard. The question is not only 'Is this working and should we continue, or change' but also 'Are we performing in an honorable and holy way?'"[16] Adherence to this higher standard, especially when it proves risky or costly, is often a source of stress for congregations. Just as human life and culture would be greatly diminished were every individual to ply a lucrative trade or forsake the risky life of artistry for a sure wage, the gospel would be less well or fully served by congregational uniformity, even with the promise of institutional vitality, financial stability, and the wholesale broadcast of Christianity's message.

What do we need to maintain our commitment and to fulfill our life as a community? Why are we here? In assessing rewards and goals, we must discern those rewards and goals truly consistent with Christian faith, teaching, and gospel. This is by no means simple in our North American context, which espouses a gospel of material success—and an inflated one, at that. It may be that because my own experience of ministry has been largely within very small communities of believers that I have a particular bias. I am well aware of the considerable cost of maintaining the life of any community and have always been grateful for the generosity of all whose gifts made my own ministries possible. But it is also the case that the bulk of the church's ministry has been more often carried out and funded by the collective generosity of many gifts, not just its wealthy patrons, and the overwhelming majority of Christian communities throughout history have been modest in size.

The fantasy that the most impressive edifices of Christendom like the great cathedrals of Europe or their American imitations were constructed out of the need for adequate space to house weekly congregations is just that, a fantasy. After factoring in the occasional social anomaly, like America's surge of religiosity in the wake of the Great Depression and World War II, the reality is that Christian communities of modest, even meager, size have thrived for more than two millennia. They have been, as Jesus suggested his kingdom would be, apportioned throughout humankind in proportions equivalent to leaven in a loaf, a tiny portion of leaven being adequate to the whole.

> There is, of course, nothing virtuous about size. I have seen vibrant small churches and sick large ones.
> — Kevin E. Martin

The measure of "success" in ministry is now, always has been, and shall continue to be fidelity. Fidelity not only to God, but to self and neighbor. Fidelity, like integrity—of which fidelity is a core component—consists in commitment to the truth of oneself, to the reality of one's gifts, abilities, possibilities, and opportunities. This is no less true of congregations than of their individual members. This integrated commitment is manifest in a life genuinely fulfilled—filled to the brim, its fullest potentials fully realized.

In the case of individual vocation we know that such fulfillment is beyond price. It is not measured in material gain or monetary compensation. The essential element is the person's commitment to self, commitment to be true to himself or herself. This commitment to truth is profoundly religious and consistent with a Christian belief in God's essential reality as ultimate Truth. Commitment to this truth, the truth of oneself, is lifelong commitment to being fully what God has created one to be. It is "letting be" the fullness of self.

The individual's pursuit of his/her fullness consists in faithful relationship. It is manifest in a mutual trust between oneself and God expressed in a creative "letting be" and a lifelong commitment to discernment, a holy attention to the truth of one's life. That discernment, undertaken in a relationship committed to cooperation with the co-creative God, is accompanied by a trusting openness that invites collaborative action. Thus, the believer knows true vocation as a fulfilled life, a life lived in all the fullness promised to Christians and described in the gospel of John (10:10).

The same principle pertains to congregations. Each congregation has its own distinctive character, manifest in the various gifts of its members. This congregational character, like the individual self, is always relative, subject to the constant, perpetual changes wrought by life's many variables. People come and go. Even those of long tenure are changed by the exigencies of their own lives. Moreover, each congregation has "neighbors," is set within a complex context of relationships. Each congregation is only one community among many communities.

Intentional communities embrace and welcome change. They believe that God can issue more than one call to an individual or a congregation in a lifetime, thus, they are always willing to move on if something isn't working, or has run its course. Gordon Cosby has often said that in his lifetime he has seen more ministries die than preachers born. — *Paul Wilkes*

A congregation's vocation begins in cooperation with God in creative "letting be," and is manifest in a lifelong commitment to discernment, a holy attention to the congregation's character. That discernment, undertaken in a relationship committed to cooperation with the co-creative God, is accompanied by a trusting openness that invites collaborative action. The congregation's true vocation, its fulfillment, is that same fullness promised to Christians and described in the gospel of John. The promise is as applicable to Christians in the aggregate as it is to any individual believer.

While it may well be the true vocation of some congregations to excel in numerical and financial growth, individual vocation is an instructive metaphor. Yes, some individuals have pursued power and wealth for their own sakes, but the biblical scriptures do not extol such figures as exemplary. It is also the case that some inherit power and wealth. But in the main, power, privilege, and wealth are conditional; while they may be accounted a part of an individual's reality, that person's "truth," they are deemed less essential than contextual. Personal fulfillment is not manifest in the accumulation of goods or power, but rather in the uses and ends to which these resources are put.

The evidence does not suggest that Bill Gates set out to achieve his wealth. His first love—and his gifts—were manifest in pursuit of a new technology's possibilities. His own abilities and passions, and the potentiality of that technology, resulted in unprecedented wealth. The responsibility of that wealth has drastically altered Gates's own vocation. His gifts are now literally more complicated and his own discernment must take them into account, leading him into vocational paths he likely never imagined in the earlier stages of his life. That the same can, and does, happen to congregations is attested in Bill Hybels's statement regarding the phenomenal growth of Willow Creek Church, "It was never our intention to build a big church. From the very start, our vision was to just 'be' the church that God intended us to be."

Bill Gates and Willow Creek Church are notable exceptions. Most individuals and congregations realize their fulfillment differently. What does it mean, then, for a congregation to embrace its difference, to commit itself to the fullest realization of its distinction? What does congregational discernment look like?

> Practicing congregations engage in discernment, finding God's will for them both as communities and as individuals. This discernment allows them to find those specific practices to which they are called — the practices that provide coherence and meaning for their own unique stories...through a deep commitment to looking at its own special gifts and reading the needs of the community in which it finds itself. These churches have found themselves in God's story, and each one has an important and irreplaceable role to play. — *Diana Butler Bass and Joseph Stewart-Sicking*

In my own experience, congregational discernment comes slowly and incrementally. Remember that what we're considering here is relationship: relationship with God, with the self (individual and congregational), and with one's neighbor. Relationship cannot be engineered, it is organic. Congregational discernment, like its personal counterpart, is subject to progressive maturation. The child discerns differently from the youth, the youth from the teen, the teen from the young adult, and so on. And just as an individual's spiritual and emotional maturation may not always align consistently with chronological age, so might a congregation's vocational maturation vary widely. A long-established congregation with a venerable history may revert to a veritable infancy, even as a newly founded congregation may experience precocious vocational acumen far exceeding its age.

stewardship of a community

In 1982 I assumed pastoral and administrative leadership of a once-thriving campus ministry that was, when I came to it, moribund. The exercise of leadership in this context demanded commitment to a long recovery and willingness to take responsibility; I characterize this as a parental style of leadership. Like a new parent, I was learning how to be what the circumstances, in my case a vulnerable ministry instead of an infant child, was calling me to be. By the third year of my tenure the basic needs had been met. The campus ministry and I had survived the vulnerabilities and we were toddling, ready to venture.

Among the experiences of those initial years one of the most memorable and consequential was a pilot project in which I was invited to participate. A consulting firm with extensive experience with nonprofit and governmental agencies was exploring the possible application of their programs in the church. A dozen clergy from different denominations were gathered for the project. On the first day each of us was given a large tablet of newsprint and a box of markers. The assignment was to take these to our rooms and spend the rest of the evening drawing a picture of our ministry. Our drawing could be as elaborate or as simple as we wished, but the picture had to include us. We spent the remaining two days of the conference examining and interpreting each of those pictures.

What I found most interesting about the group's analysis of my own diagram was that I had pictured myself and my context without any overt religious symbols, despite the reality that I was situated in the midst of a community rich with seminaries and, as an Episcopalian, I was one of the few participants in the group from a liturgical church. My drawing was of me as host/housekeeper in a large house (which was the physical reality of our facility), at the center of a large urban university community. What emerged was a picture of hospitality, and the beginnings of a more profound understanding of both my vocation and our ministry.

In the autumn of 1985, a new deacon volunteered part-time service to our campus ministry in return for our canonical supervision of her diaconate. Her husband was a student in the medical school. Among the routine newsletters that crossed my desk I noticed a program elsewhere entitled "Medicine: The Tragic Profession," in which a panel of physicians were invited to speak candidly about their experience of loss. I suggested that the deacon confer with her husband to determine whether our interest in the topic was consistent with his and his classmates' and, if so, which doctors might be good candidates for the program. His response was encouraging, so we invited three doctors to share the panel. A member of the ministry board, a graphic artist, designed and donated beautiful, eye-catching posters that were circulated on campus. On the evening of the program we welcomed forty students of the approximately four hundred enrolled in the medical school.

The lively and informative conversation on how physicians experience loss eventually became a conversation that changed the course of our ministry. The students wanted to know why the concerns the doctors addressed that evening were not part of their curriculum, why such topics seemed forbidden in the classroom. There was no conclusive answer, but with the assistance of the doctors who were present, we determined to address it.

Three students at the program volunteered to explore the matter in conversation. I arranged to meet with them weekly for several weeks, in the course of which I asked, "If you could talk about anything that you're not talking about now, what would you talk about, and with whom would you like to have the conversation?" Questions were elicited, noted, and reduced to six, to become the foci of two programs for each of the three academic quarters. The students identified doctors and other relevant people who would engage each conversation.

The students decided that dinner meetings best met their busy schedules "since everyone has to eat, anyway." Program dates were set with attention to exams and important conflicts in the medical school routine. I offered to coordinate the administrative task of contacting speakers, who were invited to donate their time and responded generously. The graphic artist on the board designed a coordinated brochure detailing the full series and postcard-size reminders that were distributed by a student volunteer to the in-house mailbox of each medical student about ten days in advance of each program. A student was hired to prepare vegetarian meals—deemed most inclusive of religious and dietary diversity.

As the series unfolded, volunteers were solicited to plan the following year's series. Soon another "pilot" program was tried in the graduate school of business. A noted alumnus of the university who came to my attention through an interview article in the alumni magazine responded to our invitation to speak on "Philanthropy as a Vocation." He flew in at his own expense and spoke to about seventy-five students, faculty, and interested members of the university development office and the Chicago philanthropic community. His remarks were provocative and instructive, grounding the history and motivation for philanthropy in the religious heritage that spawned it. Soon we had a committee of business school students exploring programs in their professional discipline.

When a law student who was active in the local Episcopal parish learned of our initiatives in medicine and business, he asked if we might do something with his professional school. We invited him to gather a few friends and we launched the conversation and began another series of programs. Soon thereafter similar student conversations gave rise to two more initiatives, one for prospective teachers and another for prospective research professionals.

In the autumn of 1989 I met with a young man who had been referred to me by his rector. In a corporate reorganization he had recently lost his job. Not sure whether he had a call to ordained ministry, he wondered if he might work with us as a way to test his vocation. He was not overly concerned that we had no financial resources to provide compensation; he had a severance and hoped to simplify his lifestyle. We did have a modest living space within the rectory separated from my own quarters, so I offered that and he accepted.

We agreed that he should give his attention to a small group of undergraduates active in our worshipping community. He invited them to a dinner with no agenda and encouraged them to bring their friends with them. Turnout was modest, about a dozen or so. As we had done with their graduate counterparts, he asked them what was lacking from their life on campus. After several weeks of rambling conversation, the group agreed that what they really wanted was a drama company. There were nearly half a dozen theater groups on campus, but all under student direction; they wanted one that was different, one that would allow them to work with a professional director.

Moreover, they wanted to use drama as a means of exploring religious and moral themes and issues. They selected *Godspell* as their first show and hired one of the many professional directors struggling to make a mark in Chicago's theatrical community. Together, they put a new spin on this campus musical warhorse by casting an Asian Jesus and a mixed-gender, multiracial band of apostles. Their venture "lost" a modest sum, but from a budgetary standpoint, it proved a reasonable price for undergraduate programming.

The following year they produced a controversial play about living and dying with AIDS that traveled to city organizations and a suburban parish youth event. Their production of *Cabaret* came to campus amidst a season of virulent antigay harassment and proved a powerful vehicle for considering the insidious ways social and political apathy can lead to devastating moral corruption.

This thumbnail sketch of one campus ministry's gradual growth represents a stewardship of a community—in this case, students, campus, church, and community—as valuable and valued partners in a collaborative "letting be." The campus ministry's vocation emerged—was discerned—in a conversation respectful of each person's vocation. We respected that the students were there to secure an education and that this was their rightful vocational priority. Thus events were planned as a dinner hour with defined boundaries, from six to eight o'clock in the evening, to allow students and gracious panelists/speakers opportunity to attend to their own vocational commitments: study, family, and so on. We respected the students' desire to make conversation the heart of the experience, thus everything was in service to that end. We did not presume to preach to them, but invited members of their own professional community to share their common concerns in open conversation.

> The church is often seen by its members as an extension of private life rather than a bridge into the public." — *Parker Palmer*

Law students reflected on their profession with a former U.S. Attorney General, with constitutional scholars whose advice is sought by Congress and Presidents, with one of the foremost litigators in America. Business school students conversed with prominent CEOs who spoke personally and frankly of ethical challenges and responsibilities, of ecological reform and employee relations, of corporate philanthropy and accountability. Medical school students heard a dean and noted surgeon speak of his recovery from alcoholism, and listened to a pediatric oncologist tell of the role her faith plays in her daily ministrations to seriously ill children and their families. From the drama ministry, one former student went into arts administration and one of those fledgling directors now serves as artistic director of one of the nation's premier drama companies; both cite with warmth and appreciation the vocational clarity derived from their theatrical ventures with this ministry. The response of the speakers and panelists is likewise revealing. Though they donated their time and talent, many thanked us for the opportunity to share in this manner. More than one offered that it was the first time anyone in the church had ever asked them to talk about their own vocations.

The vocation to hospitality revealed in markers on newsprint gradually unfolded as I and those with whom I shared ministry lived into a vocation the particulars of which varied from day to day and year to year, and the richness of which grew deeply complex in the way fine wine matures in the cask. But by autumn 1992, many of the topics engaged in our programs had been taken into the curricula of the professional schools. Discerning this as affirmation of our previous work and intimation that our vocation was in the process of change, we abandoned the professional school programs. The students most active in the campus ministry, our core congregation, wanted to continue weekly dinners. Having worked around the scheduled events of the vocational series and having tried different nights of the week, they agreed that Thursday evening represented something of a sabbath time in their routine, an evening that fit the rhythm of their lives and encouraged the relaxation of weekly anxieties and concerns. Regularizing the schedule would make the dinners a part of their routine that could be anticipated each week and would facilitate the building of relationships. There was concern, however, that these very real assets could become liabilities if the weekly event became a gathering of a clique. In time, it would be difficult for newcomers to be integrated; and without an intentional design, there could come a time when the incentive to invite newcomers might dwindle.

That is to some extent what happened. But experience of discernment's "seasons," its ups and downs, had taught me that the cycles of feast and famine are consistent with organic life and living relationship. Periods of intense activity and assured direction are invariably followed by times of quiet. Faith and experience assure that in this life neither feast nor famine is guaranteed, each is only and always temporary. That is, perhaps, one of the most important points to be made about ministry.

+ Our designs are always temporary.

+ We must always be ready to change.

+ A living relationship with a living God demands this of us.

We ought never assume abundance, neither need we fear scarcity. I have learned to value the periods of quiet, even inactivity, as vital to discerning and living into both my own vocation and the vocations of the communities of ministry I have known. Being attuned and attentive to the rhythms of personal and institutional life encourage an appreciation of all life as God's gift, life's "fullness," including rest and reflection as well as calendar pages filled with tasks.

> In the New Testament, Jesus asks everyone to change.
> With the exception of children, Jesus insists that
> every person he meets do something and change....
> Even a cursory knowledge of history reveals that
> Christianity is a religion about change.
> — *Diana Butler Bass,* Christianity for the Rest of Us

In my own ministry experience students, faculty, staff, and I worked collegially to nurture the community God gave us, to realize a community where each person's concerns and gifts could be engaged and nurtured. Because we had no illusion that we were creating a community, or a life, we did not impose our own design, but rather engaged an intentional "letting be," a discipline of listening and interpreting, of encouraging and enacting that helped a community imagine its ministry and to bring that imagination to fruition. Like midwifery, ministry dedicated to and proceeding from vocational discernment knows the deeply filled quiet of gestation, that pregnant pause symbolized in the liturgical season of Advent. In that season, at the center of which is a woman with a most unique vocation, a whole community—the church—waits with her for God's life to be born in them, of them.

The alternating rhythms of congregational life support and sustain an ecosystem which, like all living creatures, needs periods of rest and recreation (literally, re-creation) as well as times of high energy and activity. Similarly, congregations—like the individuals who compose them—are set within the more expansive ecosystem of God's creative, created activity. Within all these systems, diversity ensures creativity. A variety of congregational communities is a natural and necessary element of systemic health and wholeness. Our experiences are specific to an urban university and community with their own distinct cultures and characteristics and a denominational campus ministry with unique facilities and governance. Each had its own constituents and history, and these experiences are set within a specific time. The following snapshots offer examples of very different congregations and their particular experiences and expressions of vocational discernment.

St. Mary's Church (not its real name) and the village in which it is situated, approximately ten miles from a major urban center, trace their origins to the 1870s. Sited at the center of the village, St. Mary's modestly proportioned building is a handsome structure, its late-Victorian motifs clearly echoing those of the stone and stucco tower across the way that serves as a landmark logo of the village. Nearby stands a much larger Roman Catholic church and school. The two churches in their visible proportions represent a demographic reality; Catholics outnumber by a significant margin their Episcopal kin. The present rector of St. Mary's was called in 1975, at which time average Sunday attendance was about seventy-five. Today, average Sunday attendance is one hundred. The numbers confirm the rector's assertion that what St. Mary's has to offer is stability, a word with particular—and in this case, intentional—resonance in Christian monasticism. Monastic stability means that the monk belongs to a particular abbey, "casts his lot with this particular group of brothers for his material and spiritual needs"; the monk "shares the community's work and joins his future to that of his monastery."[17]

Stability is evident not only as product, but in a process marked by patience. Early in his pastorate, the rector offered a Sunday morning Lenten forum that proved notably popular, simultaneously confirming the rector's vocation as a teacher and revealing what he perceived to be a demonstrable hunger for education. In response, he organized several committees charged with exploring and assessing parish education. While he attended committee meetings, he did not chair. Each committee documented their work in reports that included specific recommendations.

The Adult Education Committee requested more classes, which were offered for two to three years, until interest began to fade. There followed a recommendation for a coffee hour on Sunday morning with adult education scheduled as evening classes. Still, shuffling programs could not mask a persistent malaise. Rather than ignore that reality, integrity demanded a confrontation with the truth, painful though it be. What happened next is best related in the rector's own words, spoken at the presentation of the Community Rule of Life in May 1997:

> On the third Tuesday of September 1980, at the vestry meeting that evening, I told the vestry members that I did not believe St. Mary's could survive much longer as a conventional suburban parish; demographically there was simply no reason to have an Episcopal parish in [this location]. St. Mary's only hope, I said, was to become "radical" in the original sense of that word, that is, "back to roots." The vestry members unanimously concurred, and during the succeeding ten years the vestry—and later the Parish Council—worked to discover the unique vocation of this parish. The vocation that emerged from this decade of systematic reflection, study, and prayer was that of a secular religious community, that is, an intentional, committed, Catholic religious community whose members are nonresidential, living out in the world.

The first Adult Theology Class that had been offered in 1980 eventually grew into a two-and-a-half-year program on the Anglican faith tradition, providing a vocabulary and a framework for personal spiritual development. This course, which began as elective, was adopted as a requirement for membership on the parish vestry and is now required of any person desiring full canonical membership in the parish. Limited to classes of eight participants, as many as three groups may be meeting concurrently.

In 1985 the rector and a lay member of the parish earned the necessary certification to become mentors in Education for Ministry (EFM), a four-year theological education-at-a-distance program offered by the School of Theology at the University of the South that covers the basics of the Old and New Testaments, church history, liturgy, and theology. The rector and lay member served the parish as co-mentors of this program, which became "stage two" of the education sequence for graduates of the Adult Theology Class to continue their education. A subsequent introductory course called Canterbury Pilgrimage, a comparison of Anglicanism, Roman Catholicism, and Protestantism, was developed and offered as a bridge into the extensive adult education sequence. The six-week Canterbury Pilgrimage and a four-week sequel on "Everything You Wanted to Know About St. Mary's" now serves as orientation for newcomers and is required pre-baptismal instruction.

To this point there is little to distinguish this sequence of developments from any parish gradually developing program. One must venture into the "back story," going behind and beneath the bare facts to examine the distinctiveness of the process and the people who have grown into St. Mary's.

The rector's own vocational journey confirmed his gifts for teaching, abilities which he himself accounts and assesses as surpassing his preaching. Fidelity to his own gifts encouraged travel, observation, reflection, and a keen attention to his own learning. Among the many provocative influences that have shaped his leadership as rector, he was deeply impressed with the work of the Church of the Saviour in Washington, D.C. Founded by Gordon and Mary Cosby in 1946, this unusual expression of Christian faith and life was "progressive" long before that adjective enjoyed currency in religious circles. The Church of the Saviour represented a contrarian approach to Christian life in a postwar America on the brink of a heady religious surge that would become the standard for several succeeding generations.

We will serve you, we will be with you in the way in
which you naturally gather: We will live a little chunk
of our life where you can watch what is going on.
— from "The Origin of the Church of the Saviour"
at www.pottershousebooks.org

The single word encompassing the essence of the Church of the Saviour is *commitment*. The Cosbys, themselves deeply committed to the gospel, were equally committed to nurturing small groups of believers in a life centered in Christian fundamentals. They made their home in the Adams-Morgan section of Washington, D.C., an edgy part of the city that would become the nexus of social conflict and civil unrest in the years that followed. The location alone required of any inquirer a commitment to venture beyond the bounds of status and comfort. While successive waves of boom and bust cycled through denominational churches whose memberships and fortunes swelled and ebbed, the Church of the Saviour maintained a steady course. They were a constant witness to commitment and the stability that accompanies true fidelity.

A second powerful influence came in the course of the rector's study at the Church Development Institute, a three-year leadership training program focused on the ministry of developing the community and organizational life of congregations. He undertook the course in 1997–1999, and credits that experience with "articulating [his] intuitions and providing language and grounding" in regard to his ministry at St. Mary's. There he encountered a richer understanding of Anglicanism's deep roots in monasticism, not only in its worship but in its social structures as well. These two very different expressions of Christian faith and life found in the rector a space for conversation. Considering his own formation as a self-identified Anglo-Catholic, the cognitive dissonance of these diverse visions raised many creative questions.

Thus what began as parish education did not just produce a program of activities but grew into the instrument for nurture and maturation for this congregation in every way. It is no surprise that they eventually made ongoing formation integral to life in the parish. The people, through their own commitment and stability, embraced formation as normative and began enculturating newcomers into their life by inviting them into the process that is offered not as a requirement but as an invitation to progressive formation. In short, the congregation became a true community, an organic body.

The individual is not lost or subsumed in the process; each person's own vocational discernment is aided by a progressive nurture that offers a theological foundation and vocabulary, a supportive community for conversation enhanced by resources like EFM, which integrates the individual's life and experience in the reflective process of theological exploration. Perhaps most important is the example—the modeling—represented in the intentional discernment of the parish which raises vocational discernment into the consciousness and fabric of congregational life.

Practically speaking, membership and life at St. Mary's are varied. Just as huge churches like Willow Creek have a large number of "seeker" members whose involvement is limited to worship on Sunday morning and perhaps a few ancillary social and service activities, and a more modest "core" membership whose commitment and participation are (literally) radically different, so St. Mary's offers and expects diverse members. The congregation lays out all expectations in clear communications, including its website. Consistent with monastic stability, "St. Mary's sees each member as a coequal part of a community of committed adults with adult privileges and adult responsibilities," of which theological education and spiritual formation are seen as indispensable parts. There is a stated affirmation that "the Christian life is a lifelong process of dynamic growth, not a static state of being." The parish has "no expectation or demand as to where a person begins this journey nor even where the person may be at any given time. What is considered important is the commitment to and participation in a continuing process of growth in the Christian life and the person's God-given vocation." Commitment to community worship is expressed in expected participation in the annual celebration of Holy Week, including the Triduum—Maundy Thursday, Good Friday, and Holy Saturday—as the central priority in the church life of the members of the community.

Parish membership is clearly defined:

> A person becomes a part of St. Mary's parish community simply by becoming regular in attendance and active in its worship and life. There is no further requirement or obligation. Everyone may participate fully in the work and ministry of the parish, except for those positions for which canon law specifically requires persons to be Confirmed Communicants in Good Standing of the Episcopal Church and canonically resident in the parish. These positions include Eucharistic Ministers, Licensed Lay Homilists, delegates to Diocesan Convention, etc.

Canonical membership is equally well articulated:

A baptized person may become an Episcopalian canonically resident in St. Mary's Parish by: receipt of a canonical Letter of Transfer from another Anglican parish; if already Confirmed in another branch of the Catholic Church, by being canonically Received by the Bishop; or if Baptized but not Confirmed by a Catholic bishop, by receiving the Sacrament of Confirmation.

Care is given to distinguish canonical membership as a "specialized status [that] is optional and may be sought by those who wish to actively and intentionally develop their spiritual lives. The process involves completion of the two-year Adult Theology Class, a demonstrated commitment to weekly participation in the community life and worship of St. Mary's, the assumption of responsibility in some area of the parish's ministry, and a commitment to living out the...parish Rule of Life" which more amply defines and describes commitment to formative learning, community life and worship, and active ministry.

> The essential thing "in heaven and earth" is...that there should be long obedience in the same direction. There thereby results, and has always resulted in the long run, something which has made life worth living."
> — *Friedrich Nietzsche*

Of the one hundred or so average weekly worshippers at St. Mary's, ten percent or fewer subscribe to and live under the most extensive commitment of the Rule of Life, consonant with the Anglican principle that it be "available to all, beneficial to some, required of none." In this regard St. Mary's conforms to what Dorothy Bass and Craig Dykstra describe as a setting where people "hope to learn about life-giving patterns of life suited to the multiple complex contexts in which they now live. Joining a congregation is not the same as going into the desert," they go on to say, "but congregations do resemble monasteries in aspiring to model the way things are supposed to be in their own internal life; they aim to develop shared internal practices that are theologically sound and, indeed, continuous with communal practices of early Christianity."[18]

Despite its modest membership, and contrary to any impression that this monastic model represents a cloistered introversion, the parish supports an impressive outreach in three agencies gathered as St. Mary's Community Services Corporation:

+ A preschool, founded in 1979, provides the community with a quality, affordable preschool education based on experiential learning. Operating out of the church, it is a self-funded, nonprofit agency.

+ A housing initiative was begun in 1990 with a goal of providing affordable housing to low-income buyers by acquiring and rehabilitating distressed properties, and then offering them for sale at affordable prices. Additional services include housing counseling for low-income homebuyers both before and after purchasing a house and when they are in danger of foreclosure.

+ An eldercare program, also established in 1990, provides person-to-person contact essential to the spiritual and emotional well-being of the homebound elderly. Expanding needs of the community made it necessary to enlist the help of the churches in the parish's own municipality and in four contiguous villages. Subsidiary programs extend care to residents in retirement and nursing care facilities, provide assistance to those needing door-to-door transportation, and train caregivers to take better care of themselves and reduce the stress experienced as caregivers.

Thus in its own way St. Mary's has discerned and pursued a vocation similar to the Church of the Saviour, but bearing the unique imprint of a very different place and people. They did not attempt to impose another congregation's practices, like a template, upon their own. Instead, they took the road of integrity, the long path of deep and prayerful commitment, substantial education, and intentional discernment. *Who and what is God calling us to be, here and now, in this place? Why are we here?* The manner of congregational organization and life at St. Mary's is not for everyone. But they have discerned that it is, for now and for them, their calling.

<hr>

paying attention

In September 1997 the Episcopal Church Council at the University of Chicago devoted its annual retreat to a consultation facilitated by Trustee Leadership Development. The Council had long given priority to issues and exercises of discernment in this yearly gathering inaugurating the terms of new members to the board at the beginning of the academic year. But the time had come, they felt, to do more intensive work. So they set aside time for that purpose and engaged the services of facilitators whose guidance might assist the process, while engaging the full participation of every board member.

The design for this meeting incorporated many fine principles and exercises that have emerged for assisting boards of trustees and other groups responsible for institutional stewardship, including some of those known as Appreciative Inquiry, described by one proponent as a program that "focuses us on the positive aspects of our lives and leverages them to correct the negative. It's the opposite of 'problem-solving.'"[19] Rather than following a traditional approach to change, which is "to look for the problem, do a diagnosis, and find a solution"—a process which always results in finding problems, since we are looking for them, and amplifying them since we are paying attention to them, the Council looked for what was working in the organization. "The tangible result" of this sort of inquiry, writes Sue Hammond in her book on Appreciative Inquiry, "is a series of statements that describe where the organization wants to be, based on the high moments of where they have been." These statements are "grounded in real experience and history" and thus enables the organization "to repeat their success."[20]

Sometimes you need to reaffirm who God has made you to be, what he has called you to do and where he wants to take those with whom you serve. Interacting with group members and processing personal leadership with others from differing professions was very helpful." — *The Rev. Kerry Bowman, quoted on the website of Trustee Leadership Development (http://www.tld.org)*

In the course of our conversation, every participant was asked to share some experience of our ministry that had most engaged their interest. I told of a young intern who had been working with us. One of the board members asked about the internship—how had it come about and how had this person come to us? I shared the story related in the previous chapter, of the young man who had come to me in the autumn of 1989 asking to test his vocation, and of how simply by word of mouth, another young man asked to succeed him when the opening came. I told the story of how that position had evolved over eight years and had assisted four such young adults.

The conversation deepened as interest, and excitement, grew. Finally, one board member said, "It sounds like God is encouraging us to get intentional about this ministry." That surprising revelation marked the advent of new direction for the ministry and for my own vocation.

Over the next seven years a mentoring program for young adults seeking opportunity, guidance, and clarity in their own vocational discernment would become the centerpiece of this ministry. In four years it grew from one graduate intern to a community of ten young adults in a supervised program of activities, reflection, and spiritual direction, adults who were taking responsibility for and taking part in a vibrant community of diverse ministries in varied activities.

thoughtful habits

These stories of discernment in community are only snapshots, like a glimpse into the bakery window, where the finished products are arrayed. Missing from the picture are the many steps required to reach the window's bounty. Invisible and unheard are the workers whose labors in field and factory yielded each component in the bakery trays: the ingredients, the equipment, the skills and hours spent to bring forth each loaf, cookie, cake, pastry.

Few (if any) people are born with an aptitude for vocational discernment. They want and need help. "The spiritual dimension Americans want," write George Gallup and Jim Castelli, "includes helping them to find meaning in their lives and, for Christians, to deepen their relationships to Jesus Christ. It also includes a strong desire for information about the Bible and its meaning. While Americans want spirituality from their churches, they also want practical help. They also want their churches to help them learn how to put their faith into practice; to shed light on the important moral issues of the day; to help them learn how to serve others better and to be better parents. Americans understand that for their faith to be meaningful, it must be real and have a real impact on their day-to-day lives."[21] While we may be born with the capacity for relationship and reflection, even profound spiritual yearning, we only gradually develop the skills and cultivate the sensibilities that mature into thoughtful habits manifest in meaningful lives. Congregations—human communities of all kinds—must also cultivate those practices and nurture those habits that lead to true holiness and genuine wholeness, habits that are manifest in integrity. Communities that literally practice what they preach. Communities that, in the case of Christians, incarnate the fullness of life promised by the gospel to all God's creatures.

The foregoing examples—a parish and a campus ministry engaging discernment and articulating a vocation—came to that point of maturation over a long period and by way of a gradual process. Presumably, you have come to these pages because you or some community to which you are related (or both) are in such a process. It may be helpful and instructive to be reminded of the progressive nature of process and the patience required of growth in relationship.

While intentionality is an important (and often cited) component in personal or organizational growth, we and our culture are prone to demand quick or even immediate results. As nutritionists urge repeatedly, there is no magic bullet, no foolproof, quick-fix diet; only behavioral change can ensure safe weight loss and maintenance. The same caveat applies to discernment. Attention must be paid to maturational process. At different stages in our lives different behaviors and habits pertain.

Discerning what is required of us in any situation is not always easy. Moreover, because both we and our communities are living beings, life's variability requires that we remain open and flexible. As in all relationships, communication is essential to vocational discernment. The distribution of gifts and responsibilities, the patterns of communication and relationship must be deliberately disciplined to attain the goal of mature life—that ripe life of the gospel's promise fulfilled.

The Episcopal Church Council at the University of Chicago has known life's ups and downs, seasons of feast and famine. In 1975 a popular chaplain retired after fifteen solid years of ministry and leadership. By the time of my arrival as chaplain in 1982, the Council had suffered the weariness of a protracted seven-year period of stress. From 1975 until 1978 they worked with an acting chaplain; in 1978 they called a chaplain who remained only until 1980, leaving them angry, sad, weary, and very wary of ordained leadership—despite a prevailing local religious culture that encouraged deference to ordained authority. It was a recipe for strife. Simply establishing sufficient trust would require a long-term commitment on my part.

It was not long before we all had to face the major vocational question: What are our respective ministries? What was my ministry as the ordained leader called to this community? What was their ministry as the Episcopal Church Council?

As is sometimes the case of a ministry in crisis, a purpose was revealed—a calling discerned—not from intentional reflection so much as from insistent necessity. The physical facilities, Brent House, at the time a seventy-five-year-old building suffering at least two decades of deferred maintenance, demanded attention. The Council determined that they had to engage the issue with the Diocese of Chicago, who held deed to the property. They began to discern and live into their role as stewards of a ministry as they negotiated the renovation of the building and undertook the task of securing funds for the project.

When the restoration was completed in 1987, the question arose again: What are our ministries? They were by then a different group. Their membership was more diverse; none of the original membership who had been there at my arrival remained. They had become adept at deploying their own gifts. Among them was the graphic artist who improved the printed communications of the entire ministry; a lawyer revised the bylaws and greatly simplified them; a financial development professional negotiated the renovation process with the diocese and represented the ministry in conversations with foundations and potential donors. They were led by two graduate students, serving as co-chairs of the Council, who had been encouraged to use their own vocations in service to the ministry. Now they were encouraged to lead the ministry into its own vocation.

Parenting and partnership are as ancient as Christianity itself. Both are essential to a faith community. Each is holy. But they describe very different ways to hold one another. — *James D. Whitehead and Evelyn Eaton Whitehead*

I had completed five years as chaplain, program was expanding, and the facilities had been secured to house the programs. The Council determined to get intentional about their vocation and ministry as a board. With my encouragement, they went away on retreat and, with their co-chairs as facilitators, they examined their own ministry as a board and undertook to discern their own vocation. I absented myself from the retreat and, eventually, from many of the Council's meetings, in order that they might move beyond patterns of dependence. James and Evelyn Whitehead, in *The Promise of Partnership: Leadership and Ministry in an Adult Church,* write of "the potential of absence" noting that the absence of a resident priest often leads a community to a new realization of the abundance they possess in themselves. The potential and practice of absence, I was beginning to discern, was part of my vocation now. What would have been inappropriate at an earlier stage in our life together was now proving an important component in my ministry and the board's.

The Catechism in the *Book of Common Prayer* describes the ministry of bishops and priests as "oversight." This definition pertains to all who serve in executive leadership, who bear singular leadership responsibility in community. While pop mythology and the dictator persist in defining executive leadership as the solitary imposition of individual will, the genuine executive is a particular kind of servant.

Executive: from the Latin *executivus,* from *exsequi,* "carry out, follow up"; *ex-* "out," *sequi,* "follow"

In a diverse, dispersed community, few see or know the whole. The role of executive leadership begins with attention to this purview. In the church the executive, usually the ordained leader, serves to carry out and follow up on the ministries of a diverse community with many gifts. In hierarchical ordering the leader represents the summit of a pyramid, from which vantage she or he is granted a unique perspective of the whole, hence the descriptive "oversight, overseeing." But it is increasingly the case that even as leadership evolves from hierarchical/vertical to collegial/horizontal systems, someone must bear knowledge of the whole. Some leader(s) must occupy the centermost point in community, at the hub of radiating spokes. This is the case not only for the ordained or executive leader, but for those who share the responsibility as board, vestry, council, and so on.

As indicated in the account above, the gradual maturation of the board made demands on my own ministry and vocation. I was not so aware of this the first times it surfaced; that came with the gift of hindsight. When caught up in it, I experienced this shift in the ministry's culture as unadulterated stress from an indeterminate source. It took me some time to see that the community around me was changing and that, in turn, this was demanding change of me. I had forgotten that when a spoked wheel turns, the torque is on the hub. Though each of the spokes is in motion, the point of greatest tension is at the center. I learned to respect this tension, to enter into and reflect upon this stress, to examine it for what it had to reveal to me.

space to be

Communities of ministry need separate space and opportunity for both kinds of discernment, individual and corporate. The "potential of absence" again proved beneficial in a rector's sabbatical. A vestry retreat prior to the sabbatical led to the realization that the rector's absence for several months was not a problem to be dealt with; it was an opportunity for the parish to take its own sabbatical. A series of gatherings were planned for the period of the rector's absence, some for the vestry and others for study groups. Several Sunday mornings in the course of the sabbatical were designated for intentional preaching and post-worship conversation about this "intentional pause" in the life of the parish.

The rector in this case had just celebrated her seventh year with the parish. She was aware that in those years the life and ministry of the congregation had changed significantly. She was feeling the telltale stress. The center of her sabbatical was intentional reflection upon her own vocation. Was she being called to a new ministry elsewhere? Was she being called to renew her commitment and relationship with this congregation, and to venture into a new kind of ministry and leadership with them?

The rector was not the only person experiencing the stress of change. The vestry was changing. The variety of people, attitudes, and gifts represented changed a little each year as membership terms rotated. They, in turn, were aware of the stresses of change on the larger congregation, and of the need to address that change. In the course of their own "sabbatical," the vestry and congregation were able to devote intentional attention to these issues and to explore their meaning for their present and future life together. Upon the rector's return, they reaffirmed their commitment and began a new ministry together.

As these stories illustrate, vocation—whether individual or congregational—leads us into the new, for that is the nature of living relationship. That is also the challenge of living relationship, and the special challenge of relationship with the living God. The God who professes to make all things new invites us in each new day to venture into the uncharted territory of unfolding time. In this sense, our lives and our ministries are always new lives, new ministries. Yet every venture, even the daily entry into and engagement with the mundane, demands equipment, education, and tools. How, and with what, do we equip ourselves to meet the challenges of vocation? Furthermore, if vocation is oriented toward an unknown, unfolding life, how shall we know we are in the right way? To these questions we turn next.

chapter five

The *Whole* Church

From the outset, this book has sought a renewed commitment to the Christian discipline of vocational discernment as the foundation of all ministry, individually and collectively. Central to this project is restoring vocational discernment to the *whole* church as the most basic and essential expression of the church's mission.

To that end, I offered a perspective on the Creation narratives in Genesis that presents God as origin of creative initiative manifest primarily in a generous "letting be." God is presented not as maker or manipulator but as encourager, as loving partner who invites all things into being and gives each the heart to dare and bear all that being encompasses. Stories from my own life and experiences have been offered not as models or designs but as suggestions intended to put flesh on and breathe life into what might otherwise have been a dry skeleton of words and ideas. As such, I have attempted to extend an invitation into my own perspectives respectful of each reader's need and responsibility to explore and discern his/her own vocation.

In L. Frank Baum's familiar and profoundly theological parable *The Wizard of Oz,* Dorothy, the Scarecrow, the Tin Woodman, and the Cowardly Lion undertake a complicated quest to a distant land only to learn from their experience that what they seek is already theirs. The journey itself provides them with space and time—opportunity—to discern the truth of who each of them is. The hopes and fears evidenced in the lives and communities of Christians past and present, and the many and varied schemes offering easy solutions and securities, suggest that the lure of Oz is eternal. Individually and collectively, Christians always have to choose between following after false premises and promises, and responding to God's invitation into partnership.

> Encourage: from the Old French
> *encoragier,* from the Latin *cor:* heart

God's promise of the fullness of life is also and always an invitation into God's own capacious hospitality. There we find ample space and time—eternal opportunity—to live into the fullness of our lives. God assures us that all we seek is already ours. We are given heart, we are encouraged to be. "Encourage" is one of my favorite theological words. Literally, it means "to give heart." But practically, it means to provide opportunity to be. A Tin Woodman seeking a heart, a Scarecrow in search of a brain, a Cowardly Lion in need of courage, all led by a child in quest of happiness and all partnered in their common journey find what they seek and more in the space of a few imaginative pages, in a story. They are encouraged by each other along their pilgrimage. They are encouraged as well by a godlike wizard whose legendarily fearsome facade hides a humbled human who loses his magic only to reveal his wisdom. Thus does a childhood story become a parable of vocation, and discernment.

Vocational discernment is always a partnership. For the Christian there is no such thing as individual discernment. Vocation presumes an "other;" a call issues from some other, somewhere. For the Christian there is God, always and everywhere. Thus whether undertaken by one person or a congregation, the vocational journey demands all the tools required of any living relationship, including fidelity, grace, humor, patience, and creativity. But the essential prerequisite is attitudinal, what scripture defines as "a new heart." The discerning heart is always an open heart, whether it beats in the breast of one person or pulses at the core of a group's life. The open heart that receives and responds to the call of relationship in baptism, or any of the many manifestations that vocation may take, is always at risk of retreat and resistance, of hiding and hardening.

The vulnerability of relationship is an openhearted self-offering, a radically accessible hospitality. Yet an open heart comes neither naturally nor easily to us. Nor does our culture encourage us to risk. Any inclination I might have to such generous self-opening is offset by an innate creaturely instinct to self-preservation. This instinct too quickly escalates into selfishness. *My way or the highway. We've always done it this way.* Since our Hebrew ancestors tended to see a profound unity between head and heart, at bottom such hardheaded resistance suggests a deeper affliction, a closed heart.

A new heart I will give you, and a new spirit I will put within you; and I will remove from your body the heart of stone and give you a heart of flesh. I will put my spirit within you. *(Ezekiel 36:26–27, NRSV)*

Nor is this stubborn resistance manifest solely in a recalcitrant hold on the past; it is as frequently embodied in a vehement devotion to the latest success or stubborn conviction of some envisioned future. Whether fixated upon some revered past tradition, present practice, or promising innovation, idolatry is still deemed sin by Christians. Thus, the hardest work of vocational discernment entails constant vigilance, profound awareness of sin, and continual redemption, in oneself and in every human undertaking.

+ To what extent do we understand ourselves to be redeemed human beings living within the grace and disciplines of baptism?

+ How well do we actually know and value our gifts?

+ How well and by what means do we ascertain and respect our limitations and needs?

+ To what extent are we engaged in the local community and the extended communities of our households, workplaces, and social networks?

+ How well and by what means do we know and respect our communities' limitations and needs?

These are some of the questions the discerning person and community must host continually and congenially. The resulting conversation and critique among so many diverse voices challenges the limits of even the most generous hospitality and is a constant goad to the hardened heart.

Unless we are tuned in and our hearts are prepared, God may be sending us signals, but we may not be able to hear them. The first step is to listen. We must realize that our discernment is never complete, and we must continue to be alert for new signs that appear.
— *Grounded in God: Listening Hearts Discernment for Group Deliberations*

The capacity for surprise is one of the rewards of the open heart. And the bane of the guarded heart. The messiness common to organic life is a frustration to the heart committed to rigid order, a heart that demands control or is in thrall to fear. To cite the disciples' experience, retreat into supposed security is seldom long-lived; locked doors mean little after the resurrection. Furthermore, even the best of news, including the resurrection itself, is usually preface to a new chapter in life.

> When it was evening on that day, the first day of the week, and the doors of the house where the disciples had met were locked for fear of the Jews, Jesus came and stood among them and said, "Peace be with you." After he said this, he showed them his hands and his side. Then the disciples rejoiced when they saw the Lord. Jesus said to them again, "Peace be with you. As the Father has sent me, so I send you." (John 20:19–21)

As they and generations of believers before and since have learned, living relationship with a living God hardly ever looks or behaves as we predict, and is nearly always experienced as surprise.

---

envisioning the future

"I'm mystified by what's happened to this parish," a rector declared in response to my invitation to share his experience of discernment as it relates to his life and the life of his congregation. In the eight years of his tenure, attendance at Sunday services had grown from an average ninety to one hundred twenty to just over three hundred. The 1950s physical plant had been significantly upgraded, the worship space reoriented, and a new custom pipe organ installed. Energy was abounding and evident in a growing number of programs and activities.

We began to reflect on the parish's history. A merger of two congregations, each with its own distinct identity, took place in the early 1960s. Twenty years later some members still identified themselves as having been a communicant at one or the other prior parish, often in defense of a particular attitude or preference; the merged congregation still had not yet forged a single identity. Then, around 1980, a succession of three-year rectors began. The first was a man nearing retirement, a priest whose frequent references to his previous parish, often implying its superiority, betrayed his disappointment with his present congregation. Nor did he disguise his dislike of the edgy urban neighborhood that grated against every happy memory of the affluent and picturesque suburban village he'd left behind. Like a depressed person in the family system, the rector's unhappiness pervaded. He retired after three years and returned to the community of his previous happiness.

In happy contrast, his successor was young and seemed pleased to have been called to the parish. His gifts were aligned with the general membership of the church. Well-educated and articulate, his vitality enlivened the congregation. Under his leadership membership grew, staff were added, and significant progress was made. But only three years into his pastorate, he was called to a new ministry. His departure after so swift a rise precipitated an equally dizzying dive as the congregation grieved his leaving. Though unspoken, the evidence suggested a deep sadness, the kind associated with love lost, a genuine heartbreak following an intense courtship broken just at the point of abiding love and trust, the kind of failure and disappointment that leads to nagging questions of self-worth in the one left.

After an interim a new rector was called, entering a community still in pain, confusion, and self-doubt. This priest was quite different from his predecessor. Quiet and gentle in demeanor, his calm manner perhaps prolonged the congregation's brooding. In the third year of his tenure, the community's dynamics suggested alternating fear that this rector, like the previous two, would "leave" them—or that he would not. He persevered, breaking the cycle of "abandonment," but in the remaining three years of his pastorate the congregation continued to decline, reaching the lowest ebb in its history. The interim that followed was protracted and the announcement of the current rector's call was met with relief.

As we continued to explore the congregation's growth in the past eight years, the rector agreed that reflection on the parish's history and dynamics has been important. We spoke of the ways such reflection deepens one's understanding of how and why discernment can eventuate in a right "fit," of how the mutual "conversation" between a congregation's vocation and its rector's vocation contribute to a "flow" of life, a movement of multiple vocations together that is like the life-giving movement of river water—to use a biblical metaphor particularly powerful to a people and religion accustomed to desert terrain—and reiterated in the baptismal liturgies.

"Fit" is important," affirmed the rector. "I felt called to be here, that we've been called to be together." An extrovert, this priest has attracted and encouraged an extroverted leadership in general, sometimes eliciting capacities for extroversion from members who had not previously discovered or expressed these gifts. Neither introversion nor extroversion is in itself particularly advantageous or deleterious, but balance is part of that "fit" and "flow."

Both the rector's history and the congregation's contribute to their experience of discernment and of living into their vocation. The rector was prepared for this ministry by his previous experience, affirming that no experience is ever wasted, that vocations have "flow." Attention to his own vocational trajectory is evident in this rector's reflection on his discernment and his congregation's.

"A parish does well by building on its strengths," he says he learned at National Training Labs, where he first encountered the principles of Appreciative Inquiry. Experience of conflict in a previous parish led the rector to seek training specific to issues of diversity, to improve his skills and help him better understand conflict, and to equip himself for more substantive reflection, especially in circumstances where the natural inclination is to instinctive, defensive reaction.

> Specialized knowledge and technical skills can be important contributors to achievement in many arenas. However, self-awareness, skills in dealing effectively with other people and knowledge about the fundamentals of human behavior are characteristics that distinguish the truly successful in business, in community settings and in personal relationships. — *National Training Labs Institute, www.ntl.org*

He recognized very quickly that music is a particular strength of this parish. "Even from the beginning, there was a strong and devoted choir of at least twenty up front," he says. "Today there are often forty to fifty and, on special occasions, as many as sixty-five. And the parish has a new organ, a significant but worthwhile investment." Music and its liturgical context were significant factors in the first strategic plan for the parish. The purchase of the custom pipe organ and reconfiguration of the worship space in preparation to receive the instrument and realize its potential energized the congregation and changed it, too. This done, the time came to give attention to the congregation's identity.

The rector's coming out was a significant part of his own vocational journey to wholeness, and was well behind him by the time he arrived at the present parish, who called and welcomed him and his partner as a gay couple. Coming to terms with his sexuality, a process provoked and exacerbated by crisis in a previous church, was an essential component in his personal discernment. Living with and into the truth of his own life without fear, in faith that "lets be," was not a solitary undertaking. He cites as very helpful a "support group" of professional colleagues whose companionship and collective wisdom assisted him. Too, the rector's professional orientation gradually changed from clericalism to collegiality. In subsequent ministries, the rector has helped congregations find their own identity, a process that demands honesty in the leader, as well as fidelity and commitment—trust—built with the community.

As the congregation changed in composition, every aspect of its life was affected, including styles of worship and music long appreciated. A more diverse congregation meant the need for more diverse expression in the community's worship. Like an adolescent experiencing radical change in his/her body, the congregation met every change with a commingling of fear and excitement. The rector and vestry devoted a lot of time to reminding themselves of what the parish is good at, what the parish values. Situated in a racially mixed urban community with a rich collection of nationalities and ages, that diversity only grew as more came into its doors. The parish embraced diversity as a core component of its identity and made commitment to diversity a cornerstone of its self-identity: "Newcomers and visitors are expected. We welcome orthodox believers and skeptics, people of all races and cultures, people of all classes, abilities, and sexual orientations, without imposing on any the necessity of changing to be part of our worship and community life!"[22]

As the parish became more sure of its own identity, it communicated more honestly to the membership what kind of community it was. Some chose to leave. "The vestry doesn't hand-wring," says the rector. "They are really well self-differentiated. When people leave, we understand and wish them well. If they didn't find a fit, they needed to go elsewhere." People in the parish comment on the rector's integrity, his stability, consistency, authenticity—that he's the same person, no matter the context in which one meets him. The influence of his modeling is manifest in parish leadership that is increasingly clear about what they stand for. For example, a change in worship schedules (a real stress magnet in most parishes) created some unhappiness. The rector expressed his concern about this unrest at a vestry meeting, but was assured by the vestry. Don't worry, stay the course, they counseled. They retained clarity under pressure and eventually the change was incorporated.

"Organic development is hard," says this rector, "because organic development is not linear." Time in vestry meetings is devoted to reflection; meetings of approximately an hour and a half to two hours will include up to forty-five minutes in reflection, sometimes in Bible study. "The quality of the vestry's life affects the whole parish," he offers. "People want to be on the vestry because so many have experienced it as positive." Annual vestry retreats have been organized around varied programs, but in general the vestry spends a lot of its time and energy in reflection on the church's identity, and their identity as leaders within the parish. And they imagine— envision—their congregational future. Imagining, or envisioning, is distinguished from "visioning" or "having a vision." The latter most often connotes a design or program conceived and imposed by someone(s) other than those enlisted to carry it out. The "architect" of the design may be quite imaginative and even somewhat collegial, at least in theory, but those contracted and subcontracted to carry out the plan or execute the design usually work within bounds. Like hierarchical interpretations of Creation, partnership in this model is hardly mutual or equitable. In visioning, imagination is limited to the instigator, who then projects the vision outward and "sells" it to others (or not).

Envisioning is different, and integral to vocation. The prefix *en* means "in, into" and thus suggests invitation, entry into imagination. While visioning projects, envisioning invites. Envisioning makes space and time, provides opportunity, beckons one into imagination where one can play, be creative in both anticipation and participation. The child who sees a firefighter or a ballet dancer imagines what it might be like to be a firefighter, a ballet dancer. The child enters imaginary space and inhabits the imagined role. The ability to see a variety of genders and colors in various roles increases the opportunity and likelihood of a young person's imagining. At least one of the gifts of women's ordination is the incarnate image of a female presider at the altar. Many a story has been recounted of little girls grown to womanhood who deferred or denied a vocation to ordained service simply because they had never seen a woman in that role. And of those whose first experience of seeing a female presider opened a door into imagined possibility and eventual vocation.

Similarly, a lack of younger clergy and lay leadership in congregations conveys the visual message that liturgy is the province of age. What does it say to children, youth and young adults that they can see youthful professionals in hospital, policing, government and a host of public domains, but that in church leadership, they are largely absent? With notable exception, they are not ordained, not in lay leadership, and are even marched out of worship to a place removed lest they contaminate the peace.

We imagine ourselves into our vocational roles, both in work and love. Children can and do still "play house," emulating sometimes with hilarious results the actions of adults as they seek to imagine the roles they may eventually grow into. The ability to envision—to both imagine and inhabit the imagined—is an invaluable dimension of discernment. Recall how often imagining preceded realizations in your own life, how within the span of your own imagining you were provided space and time both to anticipate and participate in your own unfolding being.

Similarly, congregations imagine themselves into their vocations. As the foregoing story suggests, attention to vocation can be a powerful and positive component in congregational vitality. When those in leadership are mindful of their own vocational discernment and sensitive to the larger community's need for vocational clarity, a mutual partnership may emerge.

There is also a cautionary element to this story; in seeking ordained leadership, attention to vocation and discernment can make a significant difference in outcomes. Many a congregation has declared in a profile or prospectus, "We want to grow!" only to prove itself committed to its familiar past and threatened by change when confronted by the realities of genuine expansion. This "bait and switch" has trapped more than a few clergy, call committees, vestries, and congregations in volatile conflict.

> All who believed were together and had all things in common; they would sell their possessions and goods and distribute the proceeds to all, as any had need. Day by day, as they spent much time together in the temple, they broke bread at home and ate their food with glad and generous hearts, praising God and having the goodwill of all the people. *(Acts 2:44–47)*

A more thoughtful discernment might place less emphasis on the journey or destination and give more attention to the vehicle in the moment. Not who do I want to be, but who are we, who am I now? Not where do we want to go, but where are we, where am I now? An honest assessment of one's gifts makes for a more stable relationship, and the prospect for growth. In the story related above, a congregation that envisioned itself as welcoming diversity and a rector who was forthright about his own gifts and personhood were committed to partnership and mutual discernment. In that relationship each makes space and opportunity for the other to be. Each is invited into the life of the other, truly living into the fullness of the apostolic life described in Acts 2, expanding commonality beyond material things to a shared life, beyond economics to vocation.

In this kind of mutuality, discernment is intentional, a discipline, a way of life. Within such a committed partnership, trust encourages honesty and allows the truth to be spoken in love. If we imagine ourselves untalented, inept, and unattractive, odds are we'll be all three, at least until our imaginings are challenged. Conversely, if we imagine ourselves capable, gifted, and personable, chances are good our lives will flow in that direction. A parish that defines itself as a community of radical hospitality is constantly imagining what that means for itself. Thus tending to even the most basic functions of parish life, all is examined and imagined to be consistent with congregational identity. This is authentic living.

Authenticity: from the Greek
authentikos, "genuine"

Unlike congregational development that centers on behavior modification, the belief that "if we only do this, then that will happen," the life of the parish profiled above proceeds from its discernment of itself, and letting itself be what it truly is. When I have asked those who have come to the congregation in recent years why they have made this their community, they most often cite the parish's authenticity. The parish is what it is—which is consistent with the authenticity of a God who bears the name "I am Who I am." This kind of authenticity drew people to Jesus. It continues to draw people to Jesus, in the church.

God makes community

Many surveys of American culture, and the churches within it, indicate that loneliness is widely experienced in modern American life and that many people desire a community. Yet attempts to create community frequently fail, perhaps because they are essentially flawed in their assumption that community can be "made." Indeed, the attempt to "make" community can undermine community. Family, however configured, remains one of the most basic units of "community." A household is and has long been respected as community in its most elemental form. Despite the emphases upon "family" in many contemporary congregations, many of the structures of congregational life contrive to keep families apart. Activities are not centered in the home, but demand that families come to church, where they are segregated by age and/or interest. The natural community made of kinship and commitment is disrupted by a competing community called church.

We do not "make" community; God makes community. The church discovers and celebrates this community, the ultimate community for Christians, the community of God's making: the community of all creation. This community, affirmed in the first confessional premise of every Christian creed, is the community that shares a common genesis in God, maker of all things. This community is only gradually revealed, and not easily. This revelation is hardly forthcoming in a culture of isolation, competition, independence, and autonomy. Yet, for the Christian, discernment is rooted and vocation is lived in this fundamental unity all creation shares in God. In the unity between God and humankind revealed in Jesus and manifested in the Spirit that flows out of that living relationship between God and all that God has made (and continues to make), the faithful continually seek and find that unity everywhere, in everything and in everyone. Discernment and vocation begin with the recognition of this community that is by no means self-evident.

For the creation waits with eager longing for the revealing of the children of God.... We know that the whole creation has been groaning in labor pains until now; and not only the creation, but we ourselves, who have the first fruits of the Spirit, groan inwardly while we wait for adoption, the redemption of our bodies. (Romans 8:19, 22–23)

The church, and its leadership particularly, easily and frequently assume a quality of relationship that does not necessarily exist. Owing perhaps to our own cultural mythologies of affectionate images of close-knit communities, of extended generations gathered in pews, their hearts warmed by the refrains of romantic hymns extolling the blest ties that bind hearts in Christian love, we forget that when we gather we are, for the most part, a company of strangers. In truth we know little or nothing of each other. Modern families are no exception. Rarely gathered at table and seldom engaged in real conversation, in most homes a "family" night or occasion often centers on a television set or multiple computers scattered in separate rooms under the same roof.

Kinship and social structures common to previous generations have all but dissipated in American culture and experience. Nostalgia blurs reality; earlier generations also knew displacements and disintegration. Families were divided by death and practical logistics; sheer distance between widely scattered farms and migratory labor patterns, often necessitated by economic hardship, had their own stressful effects. The relatively short-lived homogeneity that accompanied the burst of large-scale home building in densely populated suburbs gave rise to a similar growth spurt in churches. But this development was exceptional. In less than half a century, America has reverted to social fragmentation and individual isolation. Sociologist Robert Putnam characterized this atomization in his aptly titled book *Bowling Alone,* in which he documents the realities every congregation faces: a culture less inclined to adhere around the structures of voluntary association, family, or even friendship.

In truth, there are many benefits to this change, not least the increases in individual and family income that make such independent living possible for more people. But there are obvious deficits, too. Easy credit fosters the illusion of affluence; access to information fosters the illusion of knowledge; ease of communication fosters the illusion of relationship; and sheer density fosters the illusion of community. Where once one might do the hard work of discernment toward clarity and make the choices of one's life within networks of family and friendship, where "clearness committees" were as close as family and friends who constituted our informal yet important councils of advice, today we must be far more intentional in seeking them out. I have often noted of young couples in premarital interviews that they live far from family, unaware of their next door neighbors. Their daily friendships are formed in separate workplaces, their little free time is divided by individual interests and a right devotion to nurturing their marriage. Who would ever know them and relate to them as a couple? At least a church congregation could fulfill that role and offer that invaluable perspective in their lives.

How do we nurture the kind of communal life upon which discernment depends, within which vocation is fulfilled? Commitment to the hard work of discovering and excavating community from the cultural accretions beneath which it is disappearing is the difficult, countercultural labor demanded of us.

<hr/>

clarity in brokenness

It is neither accident nor invention that so much of this book has emphasized conversation, and the time and commitment conversation requires. Conflict has badgered the Episcopal and other churches for centuries. In the first decade of the twenty-first century, our Anglican Communion is fractured and perilously close to broken. Still, even (sometimes especially) in brokenness God's truth is more clearly and fully revealed.

Decisions made in recent years by the Episcopal Church and by the Anglican Church of Canada in 2003, primarily related to issues of sexual norms and practice, provoked a crisis eventuating in the formation of a special commission. Established by the Archbishop of Canterbury to explore the precarious unity of the Anglican Communion, the Windsor Report was their product. The opening sentence of the report's foreword leaves no doubt that the central issue is vocation, and the task, discernment: "What do we believe is the will of God for the Anglican Communion?"

The Windsor Report was received by the Diocese of Chicago, and assigned to a diocesan task force for study and recommendations. In 2004 I was asked by my bishop to co-chair this task force; my colleague and counterpart, George, is rector of a congregation in a distant suburb. Politically and spiritually we represent the divergence of experience and conviction in our diocese and the larger church. George and I hardly knew one another. Our acquaintance was limited largely to the occasional professional clergy meeting, usually over a hundred clergy gathering in a large room, with little opportunity or inclination to enlarge their friendships. With only a vague notion of our task, we decided that before anything else, we needed to meet. So we met for lunch. With no other agenda before us, we simply shared with each other the stories of our lives and, particularly, of our calls to and experiences of our ministries. Three hours later we departed, with the awareness that in nearly ninety-five percent of our lives we shared common ground. While the remaining five percent of difference represented a significant separation, it was not so vast a fissure that we could not reach across it.

The experience was so important to us that we designed the year-long deliberations of the task force around it. All our work would begin with and be grounded in informed relationship with one another. The most significant learning and recommendation of the task force grew out of this experience: an intentional commitment to relationship was recommended to the diocese. It was recommended that every congregational vestry and committee, every diocesan commission and diocesan convention commit to the nurture of relationship as priority and prerequisite to deliberation and business.

> How do you understand a world in which the only material form is that of relationships, and where there is no sense of an individual that exists independent of its relationships? That was the gift of the quantum worldview. It said there are no independent entities anywhere at the quantum level. It's all relationships. That was something that made a lot of sense to how we were starting to think about organizations—as webs of relationships. — *Margaret Wheatley*

Challenging assumptions and refusing to indulge them is a recurring theme in vocational discernment. The power and tendency of assumptions to become self-fulfilling is evidenced in personal and institutional vocation. Many a person's vocation has been discerned, discovered, when overweening assumptions were challenged. The person diverted from a love of music or art at some early age, crushed by some parent or teacher who declared "You have no talent!" The poet whose love of words was subsumed beneath the familial expectation that she would follow her mother into medicine, or that he would naturally take over his father's business. The person who so interiorized a lifetime of negative social messages that she despaired of any meaningful vocation for fear that she would never be "good enough."

Congregations, too, have lives and histories. They have identities and are as susceptible as any living creature to those forces that shape those identities. A congregation's self-image, like any person's, is a significant factor in discernment. While there are some congregations who think far too little of themselves, who need encouragement to identify and cultivate their best assets, it is far more common to find congregations that sincerely believe they are other than what they truly are.

For example, in her book *Welcoming Children,* Joyce Mercer shows how faulty a congregation's evaluation of itself can be, how many a congregation that considers and even promotes itself as welcoming to children may in truth be otherwise. By examining congregational life and practices from the perspectives of children—by actually inviting children to critique the community—she offers valuable insights into how and why a congregation might actually include children in the fullness of its life. The latter point—why—is particularly instructive. Mercer believes that children have a vocation within the life of the congregation:

> Children are gifts from God not because they are carefree and bring delight at all times. They are gifts from God because God has a purpose for children in the world. God is calling children to lead in the struggle of faith as they point to what needs to

happen for justice to reign. Children are thus part of God's redemptive activity, showing the church how to welcome the unwelcome of the world.[23]

This claim may be rightly extended to each member of every congregation. Indeed, it is an essential component of any congregation's discernment. To neglect it is as egregious as overlooking the essentials of one's own life in assessing personal vocation.

Why, we might ask, has God called this person, or that one, to share our life? That's a question that most often arose in my own experience just when I was struggling to deal with a particularly demanding situation or person. It seldom came to mind with calm grace, but was more often the exasperated expression of exhausted patience.

Consider Shirley (not her real name), an obviously bright young woman who was hardly remarkable in a roomful of graduate and college students. We met early in my long tenure as a chaplain at the University of Chicago. Over the years, however, her distinction clarified around a noticeable psycho-social distress. On some occasions she was alert and incisive, revealing an excellent, well-educated mind. But on other occasions, she was agitated, fidgety, and defensively reclusive. At worship among a small group gathered in an intimate space her physical restlessness was especially apparent and distracting.

Shirley was nearly always visibly appreciative of what she shared in the company of those gathered for whatever activity brought us together. And she was unfailingly faithful in attendance; thus we saw her many personality quirks. Over the span of nearly twenty years, I pieced them together. Shirley's keen mind and promising career had been interrupted by mental illness. Her vocation had been one of challenge. One year in particular stands out. When she lost a job and was unable to pay her rent, she was evicted from the rooming house where she lived modestly. Unable to afford the patented drugs that helped maintain her mental and emotional equilibrium, she consulted her doctor and reverted to a less expensive medication with harsher side-effects. When she called me for help, I knew she had exhausted her resources. I asked her what she needed. She had located a small apartment and needed a security deposit and the first month's rent. We discussed how she might secure it. I placed a preliminary call to a diocesan agency to verify her need and vouch for her; then I referred her to make the request and arrangements herself. With a modest amount of money granted by the agency, Shirley secured a new home and was encouraged. She found a new job, one that allowed her to use her considerable academic gifts in a setting congenial to her limitations. She returned to her medications and soon her life was back on track again.

A few years later, seated at the dining table with half a dozen others of our community, the discussion turned to biblical accounts of miraculous healing. Someone offered the perspective of John Dominic Crossan, who distinguishes between curing and healing and suggests that whether Jesus actually rid a person of disease was less certain than Jesus' ability to restore a person to full membership and participation in whatever relationships had been severed by illness.[24] Jesus breached the boundaries society and illness had erected around the diseased person. Removing the boundaries, restoring the person to relationship: whether the person was cured or not, Jesus had made each person whole.

Shirley listened intently, then sat erect, her posture signaling her desire to speak. As everyone's attention turned to her, she related in outline her long relationship with this fluid community, of how she had often been ill and sometimes difficult because of her disease, but she had always been welcomed, fed, befriended in this place. Then quietly, and with a warm smile, she offered the simple benediction, "Thank you, all of you, for making me whole."

The wholeness was and is mutual. Shirley's vocation to our community, and our vocation to her, were also and obviously part of God's redemptive activity. Her words articulated the gratitude of each of us around that table, for we had all found wholeness in our own lives within the church. All along the way, in different ways and varying degrees, Christians singly and in congregations had quietly made us whole, had provided us space and opportunity to be. They had let us be all that God has made, is making, us to be.

The New Testament writers address the issue of diverse gifts in community in Hebrews, Ephesians, 1 Corinthians, and Romans. Each instance suggests that maintaining that diversity harmoniously has been a challenge to the church from its inception. But that challenge is also of the essence of the church and central to its vocation. Being the place that offers space and opportunity to let each person be all that God has called them to be, being a new creation set solidly in the midst of an older, ongoing creation is central to a biblical understanding of the church's vocation, central of being a whole church.

O God of unchangeable power and eternal light:
Look favorably on your whole Church,
that wonderful and sacred mystery. (BCP 515)

I am mystified, the rector declared. A good word for vocation, and an appropriate place to conclude. For vocation is ultimately a gift, born of the life God has given us when we let that life be all that God intends for it and in it. When that happens, we stand at the threshold of mystery, face to face with the partner who loves us we know not how or why, but who loves us in life shared. We are properly and humbly mystified, beckoned to the verge of that mystery which is our life, beckoned by the source of that life who is Mystery, beckoned to stand if only momentarily in that place where both find union. From this vantage point we see how much more is accomplished than we ever asked or imagined, and know the fullness of life promised in that promise fulfilled.

A Guide for Discussion

You may of course read the books in this series on your own, but because they focus on the transformation of the Episcopal Church in the twenty-first century the books are especially useful as a basis for discussion and reflection within a congregation or community. The questions below are intended to generate fruitful discussion about how members of the group have experienced vocational discernment, not only within the institutional church, but also more broadly in all aspects of their lives. The questions therefore focus both on what has been helpful and what has been lacking; on how the church has been supportive and where it has fallen short. They also seek to balance the personal with the corporate experience of vocational discernment.

Each group will identify its own needs and will be shaped by the interests of the participants and their comfort in sharing personal life stories. Discussion leaders will wish to focus on particular areas that address the concerns and goals of the group, using the questions and themes provided here simply as suggestions for a place to start the conversation.

chapter one

Why Am I Here?

Portaro notes that any process of vocational discernment must begin and end with the BIG question, "Why am I here?" How we answer this essential question involves our discernment of the commitments we make in our lives: the kind of work we undertake, the commitments we make to others, the "shape and meaning" of our lives (p. 4).

- ♦ Over the course of your life, how have you answered the question, "Why am I here?"

- ♦ What is your story of vocational discernment?

- ♦ When the "shape and meaning" of your life has not been clear to you, what or who has helped you clarify why you are here?

♦　♦　♦　♦　♦

Reread the Prayer Book Catechism's answer to the question, "What is the ministry of the laity?"

Q. What is the ministry of the laity?
A. The ministry of lay persons is to represent Christ and his Church; to bear witness to him wherever they may be; and, according to the gifts given them, to carry on Christ's work of reconciliation in the world; and to take their place in the life, worship, and governance of the Church. *(BCP 855)*

- ♦ What are some of the ways you carry out these ministries in the world and the church?

- ♦ How would you answer this question, if you were writing a Catechism for the twenty-first century?

How Did We Get Here?

In this chapter Portaro contrasts the common understanding of vocation as "call and response, or order and
obedience" with vocation as a divine "letting be" (p. 25).

+ Does this distinction make sense to you? In what
  ways have you understood God's call as something
  to which you should respond or obey?

+ In what ways have you experienced God's call as
  sharing in God's "creative impulse" within a relationship of love?

+ How have you discerned ways in your life to be a
  co-creator with God?

♦   ♦   ♦   ♦   ♦

Portaro states that "True discipleship not only dirties the
hands, it breaks the heart, opens the mind, and stretches
the nerves, as all good learning does." He goes on to say
that at the heart of such discipleship is a "very dangerous
conversation" that takes place within our intimate relationship with God (p. 42).

+ In what ways and in which places have you
  discovered "true discipleship" in your life,
  congregation, or community?

+ How has this discipleship—this "good learning"—
  changed you?

+ In what ways is discipleship part of a "dangerous
  conversation" for you?

chapter three

God's Gift to the World

"Appreciation of vocational discernment as a lifelong expression of baptism," Portaro notes in this chapter, "acknowledges the various stages of human maturation as integral to personal vocation" (p. 54).

+ What are some of the distinctive gifts of the stages of life—the unique gifts of children or teens, young families or people at midlife, the elderly?

+ How are those gifts nurtured and discerned in the congregation? How are they silenced?

+ How have you been able to live your vocation at various stages of personal development?

+ + + + +

Portaro believes that a renewed theology of vocation that places our worth not in "utility" but in our origin in God offers us the opportunity to oppose those cultural biases and religious theologies that "equate spiritual and vocational fulfillment with financial success, social status, and political power" (p. 64).

+ How does your congregation support the vocational discernment of people whose lives are marked by limitations of some kind?

+ In what ways does your congregation affirm (or deny) the worthiness of every person in its worship, congregational life, and ministries?

+ How is your vocation shaped by your own limitations? How might those limitations enhance your vocation?

chapter four

Why Are *We* Here?

In this chapter Portaro speaks of the experience of "flow," which he describes as "the integration we experience when all aspects of life are functioning at maximum capacity and efficiency, when one is fully engaged, fully focused, and fully available to the moment" (p. 81).

+ When have you experienced "flow" in your life? When have you had a sense of "flow" in the life of your community or congregation?

+ What contributed to these experiences and made them possible?

+ What interrupted the "flow" or caused it to end? Was the disruption perceived as obstruction or opportunity?

+ + + + +

Portaro describes congregational discernment as a process that "comes slowly and incrementally" because it is based in relationship with God, self, and neighbor. He goes on to note that the vocation of a congregation, like the vocations of individuals, are "subject to progressive maturation" and development (p. 86).

+ How would you describe your congregation's current stage of vocational development?

+ How does your congregation discern God's call as a community?

+ In that discernment process, what questions need to be asked, and by whom? Who needs to hear the answers?

chapter five

The *Whole* Church

In this chapter Portaro states: "We imagine ourselves into our vocational roles, both in work and love." He goes on to say, "The ability to envision—to both imagine and inhabit the imagined—is an invaluable dimension of discernment" (p. 122–123).

+ When have you imagined yourself into a new way of living, or a new vocational role?

+ Who or what encouraged and sustained you as you turned your imaginings into reality?

+ When have you or your congregation been unable or unwilling to envision a new future? Why?

♦ ♦ ♦ ♦ ♦

Also in this chapter Portaro poses a fundamental question: "How do we nurture the kind of communal life upon which discernment depends, within which vocation is fulfilled?" He goes on to assert that "commitment to the hard work of discovering and excavating community from the cultural accretions beneath which it is disappearing is the difficult, countercultural labor demanded of us" (p. 127–128).

+ What response might your congregation make to the question Portaro asks?

+ How might your congregation undertake the "hard work" of discerning its unique vocation in this place, at this time? In what ways might that work be countercultural?

+ What might encourage that work of discernment? What could hinder it?

Resources

internet

A reminder is in order that the World Wide Web is a continually changing resource. New treasures are added every minute and trusted ones can disappear in a flash— or a keystroke. The use of a reliable search engine like Google and thoughtful keyword(s) often yield many good results.

www.resourcingchristianity.org
www.wabashcenter.wabash.edu
   (see especially the "resources" link on main page)
   By far, these are the best comprehensive sites for readers of this book. If you can't find what you're looking for here, it either doesn't exist or probably isn't worth finding!

http://hendrik-kraemer-haus.de/kraemer-e.htm
   An introduction to and bibliography of the work of Hendrik Kraemer

organizations

This list is suggestive, not exhaustive. The websites cited above offer links to many other organizations that provide educational opportunities and consulting services.

THE ALBAN INSTITUTE
www.alban.org

An independent center of learning and leadership development with a focus on congregations. Located in greater Washington, D.C., Alban is a not-for-profit, membership organization that develops and shares knowledge through consulting, publishing, research, and education programs.

THE COALITION FOR MINISTRY IN DAILY LIFE
www.dailylifeministry.org

An international network of Christians and their organizations committed to fostering the affirmation and practice of ministry in daily life by all followers of Christ through its quarterly publication called LayNet, annual weekend consultations, Internet sharing groups, and periodic projects responding to special opportunities.

LISTENING HEARTS MINISTRIES
www.listeninghearts.org

Offers programs united under the common theme of spiritual discernment and designed to help people, both as individuals and as members of a group, recognize and respond to God's call. Some are for a relatively wide audience. Others are more narrowly tailored to meet the particular needs of a specific group or a specific set of circumstances.

MINISTRY DEVELOPMENT COUNCIL
www.ministrydevelopment.org

Exists to strengthen and support organizations and individuals who serve the churches in promoting healthy and effective leadership for ministry. Serves as a catalyst for addressing leadership

issues facing the churches, including the assessment, develop-
ment, and support of candidates and church leaders in spiritual
formation, vocational discernment, and career counseling.

RENOVARÉ

www.renovare.org

A not-for-profit corporation organized under the laws of the
state of Kansas (USA). RENOVARÉ is committed to working
for the renewal of the Church of Jesus Christ in all her multi-
faceted expressions and describes itself as "Christian in commit-
ment; International in scope; Ecumenical in breadth."

TRUSTEE LEADERSHIP DEVELOPMENT, INC.

www.tld.org

A member-supported organization dedicated to advancing
boards and leaders of not-for-profit and community-based
organizations through programs and services.

books

Alphonso, Herbert, Sheila Fabricant Linn, Matthew Linn, and
Dennis Linn. *Discovering Your Personal Vocation: The Search for*
Meaning Through the Spiritual Exercises. Mahwah, N.J.: Paulist
Press, 2001.

Badcock, Gary D. *The Way of Life: A Theology of Christian*
Vocation. Eugene, Ore.: Wipf & Stock Publishers, 2002.

Bass, Diana Butler. *Christianity for the Rest of Us: How the*
Neighborhood Church is Transforming the Faith. San Francisco:
HarperOne, 2006.

———. *The Practicing Congregation: Imagining a New Old*
Church. Herndon, Va.: Alban Institute, 2004.

———. *Strength for the Journey: A Pilgrimage of Faith in*
Community. San Francisco: Jossey-Bass, 2004.

Bass, Diana Butler, and Joseph Stewart-Sicking, eds. *From Nomads to Pilgrims: Stories from Practicing Congregations.* Herndon, Va.: Alban Institute, 2005.

Beckett, John D. *Mastering Monday: A Guide to Integrating Faith and Work.* Downers Grove, Ill.: InterVarsity Press, 2006.

Dewar, Francis. *Called or Collared: An Alternative Approach to Vocation.* London: Society for Promoting Christian Knowledge, 2002.

Farnham, Suzanne G., Joseph P. Gill, R. Taylor McLean, and Susan M. Ward. *Listening Hearts: Discerning Call in Community.* Harrisburg: Morehouse Publishing, 1991.

Forrester, Kevin Thew. *I Have Called You Friends: An Invitation to Ministry.* New York: Church Publishing, 2003.

Grisez, Germain, and Russell Shaw. *Personal Vocation: God Calls Everyone by Name.* Huntingon, Ind.: Our Sunday Visitor, 2003.

Haughey, John C., ed. *Revisiting the Idea of Vocation: Theological Explorations.* Washington, D.C.: Catholic University of America Press, 2004.

Kraemer, Hendrik. *A Theology of the Laity.* Vancouver, B.C.: Regent College Publishing, 2005.

LaReau, Renee M. *Getting a Life: How to Find Your True Vocation.* Maryknoll, N.Y.: Orbis Books, 2003.

McCarty, Michele M. *Christian Vocations.* Orlando: HarcourtReligion, 2002.

Nemeck, Francis, and Marie Theresa Coombs. *Called by God: A Theology of Vocation and Lifelong Commitment.* Eugene, Ore.: Wipf & Stock Publishers, 2001.

Palmer, Parker J. *Let Your Life Speak: Listening for the Voice of Vocation.* San Francisco: Jossey-Bass, 1999.

Placher, William C., ed. *Callings: Twenty Centuries of Christian Wisdom on Vocation.* Grand Rapids: Eerdmans, 2005.

Portaro, Sam. *Crossing the Jordan: Meditations on Vocation.* Cambridge, Mass.: Cowley Publications, 1999.

———. *Sheer Christianity: Conjectures on a Catechism.* Cambridge, Mass.: Cowley Publications, 2004.

Portaro, Sam, and Gary Peluso. *Inquiring and Discerning Hearts: Vocation and Ministry with Young Adults on Campus.* Atlanta: Scholars Press, 1993.

Radcliffe, Timothy. *Sing a New Song: The Christian Vocation.* Springfield, Ill.: Templegate, 1999.

Rowthorn, Anne. *The Liberation of the Laity.* Harrisburg: Morehouse Publishing, 1986.

Schuurman, Douglas J. *Vocation: Discerning Our Callings in Life.* Grand Rapids: Eerdmans, 2004.

Schwehn, Mark R., and Dorothy C. Bass, eds. *Leading Lives That Matter: What We Should Do and Who We Should Be.* Grand Rapids: Eerdmans, 2006.

Stevens, R. Paul. *The Other Six Days: Vocation, Work and Ministry in Biblical Perspective.* Grand Rapids: Eerdmans, 2000.

Veith, Gene Edward. *God at Work: Your Christian Vocation in All of Life.* Wheaton: Crossway Books, 2002.

Whyte, David. *Crossing the Unknown Sea: Work as a Pilgrimage of Identity.* New York: Riverhead, 2002.

Wingren, Gustaf. *Luther on Vocation.* Eugene, Ore.: Wipf & Stock Publishers, 2004.

Zabriskie, Stewart C. *Total Ministry: Reclaiming the Ministry of All God's People.* Annapolis Junction, Md.: Alban Institute, 1995.

Notes and Sources

notes

1. William Stringfellow, *A Private and Public Faith* (Grand Rapids: Eerdmans, 1962), 48.
2. Verna Dozier, *In Dialogue with Scripture: An Episcopal Guide to Studying the Bible,* ed. Linda L. Grenz (New York: Episcopal Church Center, 1993), 34.
3. George Gallup and Jim Castelli, *The People's Religion: American Faith in the 90s* (New York: Macmillan, 1989), 7.
4. Didier Maleuvre, *Musings on Barbarous Beauty: A Conversation Series on Art and the Sacred,* ed. Ronne Hartfield (Cambridge: The President and Fellows of Harvard College, 2004), 98.
5. See www.listeninghearts.org.
6. Kenneth Leech, *Soul Friend: An Invitation to Spiritual Direction* (San Francisco: HarperSanFrancisco, 1992), 193.
7. Sharon Daloz Parks, *Big Questions, Worthy Dreams: Mentoring Young Adults in their Search for Meaning, Purpose, and Faith* (San Francisco: Jossey-Bass, 2002), 198.
8. Pamela Smith McCall, "All in the Family," *The Christian Century* (April 18–25, 2001), 22–23.
9. Harvard Business School publication # 9-691-102, prepared by James Mellado under the supervision of Leonard A. Schlesinger. Copyright 1991 by the President and Fellows of Harvard College.

10. Ibid., 7.
11. For a thorough and thoughtful theological perspective, consult the work of Douglas John Hall, especially his three-volume study of Christian theology in a North American context: *Thinking the Faith* (1991); *Confessing the Faith* (1996); and *Professing the Faith* (1998), all published by Augsburg Fortress.
12. Mihaly Csikszentmihalyi, *The Evolving Self: A Psychology for the Third Millennium* (New York: Harper, 1994), 3.
13. Katherine Tanner, *Jesus, Humanity, and the Trinity: A Brief Systematic Theology* (Minneapolis: Fortress Press, 2001), 15.
14. Email correspondence, dated December 5 and December 29, 2006.
15. John L. McKnight, "Why Servanthood is Bad," online at www.northwestern.edu/ipr/abcd/servanthood.html.
16. Paul Wilkes, *Excellent Protestant Congregations* (Louisville: Westminster John Knox Press, 2001), 165.
17. Quoted at http://www.saintjohnsabbey.org/beingamonk.
18. Dorothy C. Bass and Craig Dykstra, "Christian Practices and Congregational Education in Faith" from the website http://www.resourcingchristianity.org.
19. T. H. White, "Working in Interesting Times: Employee Morale and Business Success in the Information Age," in *Vital Speeches of the Day*, Vol. XLII, No. 15 (May 15, 1996); see also http://appreciativeinquiry.case.edu.
20. Sue Hammond, *The Thin Book of Appreciative Inquiry* (Plano, Tx.: Thin Book Publishing Company, 1998, 6–7.
21. George Gallup, Jr., and Jim Castelli, *The People's Religion* (New York: Macmillan Publishing Co., 1989), 253.
22. The parish's welcome statement, which appears on printed bulletins and the congregation's website, is adapted from the statement of the Center for Progressive Christianity, www.tcpc.org.
23. Joyce Ann Mercer, *Welcoming Children: A Practical Theology of Childhood* (St. Louis: Chalice Press, 2005), 256.
24. See John Dominic Crossan, *The Historical Jesus: The Life of a Mediterranean Jewish Peasant* (San Francisco: Harper, 1993). For the same material in less academic and more accessible language, see Crossan's recasting for general readership: *Jesus: A Revolutionary Biography* (San Francisco: Harper, 1995).

sources quoted

Quotations set apart within the chapters have been taken from the following books and articles.

Diana Butler Bass, *Christianity for the Rest of Us: How the Neighborhood Church is Transforming the Faith* (San Francisco: HarperOne, 2006), 24.

Diana Butler Bass and Joseph Stewart-Sicking, eds, *From Nomads to Pilgrims: Stories from Practicing Congregations* (Herndon, Va.: Alban Institute, 2005), 4.

Richard J. Chartres, "The Return of the Hidden God: Renewing our Partnership in the Gospel," The Seventh Hobart Lecture, given on September 20, 2006; www.dioceseny.org.

Kevin Thew Forrester, *I Have Called You Friends: An Invitation to Ministry* (New York: Church Publishing, 2003), vii.

Frank Griswold, *Episcopal Life* (November 2006): 23.

Grounded in God: Listening Hearts Discernment for Group Deliberations may be found at www.listeninghearts.org.

Kevin E. Martin, *The Myth of the 200 Barrier: How to Lead through Transitional Growth* (Nashville: Abingdon, 2005), 132.

Joyce Ann Mercer, *Welcoming Children: A Practical Theology of Childhood* (St. Louis: Chalice Press, 2005), 152.

Friedrich Nietzsche, *Beyond Good and Evil*, trans. Helen Zimmern (Mineola, N.Y.: Dover Books, 1997), 57.

Parker Palmer, "Practicing the Public Life in the Congregation," in *The Calling of the Laity*, ed. Verna Dozier (Washington, D.C.: Alban Institute, 1988), 79.

"Portraits of Protestant Teens: A Report on Teenagers in Major U. S. Denominations," National Study of Youth and Religion, www.youthandreligion.org/news/2005-0523.html.

Philip Sheldrake, "Discernment and Decision Making," an address to the Episcopal House of Bishops, meeting during September 2005 in the Diocese of Puerto Rico.

Phyllis Tickle, *The Shaping of a Life: A Spiritual Landscape.* (New York: Doubleday, 2001).

Margaret Wheatley, author of *Leadership and the New Science,* from an interview at www.scottlondon.com/interviews/wheatley.html.

James D. Whitehead and Evelyn Eaton Whitehead, *The Promise of Partnership: Leadership and Ministry in an Adult Church* (San Francisco: Harper Collins, 1991), 3.

Paul Wilkes, *Excellent Protestant Congregations* (Louisville: Westminster John Knox Press, 2001), 33.

Rowan Williams, "The Christian Priest Today," lecture at Ripon College Cuddesdon, 2004; text available at http://www.archbishopofcanterbury.org/sermons_speeches/2004/040528.html.

contributors

The following individuals and communities have graciously shared their stories and life with me over the course of many years in ministry.

All Saints' Church in Corpus Christi, Texas
All Saints' Church, East Lansing, Michigan
Canterbury at Southwest Texas State University and the Diocese of
    Southwest Texas
Chaplain Mark Pryce and the students of Corpus Christi College,
    Cambridge University, UK
The Campus Ministries of the Episcopal Diocese of New Hampshire
Christ Church Cathedral, St. Louis, Missouri
Canterbury Episcopal Campus Ministry at the University of
    California, Berkeley

Churches in Illinois: Calvary Episcopal Church, Lombard; Church of
Our Saviour, Chicago; Church of St. Paul & the Redeemer,
Chicago; Church of the Holy Nativity, Clarendon Hills; Church
of the Transfiguration, Palos Park; Emmanuel Episcopal Church,
Lagrange; Grace Episcopal Church, Oak Park; St. Charles'
Episcopal Church, St. Charles; St. Christopher's Episcopal
Church, Oak Park; St. Chrysostom's Episcopal Church, Chicago;
St. Elisabeth's Church, Glencoe; St. James Cathedral, Chicago; St.
John's Episcopal Church, Naperville; St. Mark's Church,
Barrington Hills; St. Michael's Church, Barrington; St. Paul's
Parish, Riverside; St. Peter's Church, Sycamore; St. Thomas
Episcopal Church, Chicago; Trinity Church, Highland Park
Episcopal Campus Ministry at New York University
Episcopal Campus Ministry at the University of Maryland
Episcopal Campus Ministry and Trinity Church, Bozeman, Montana
The Episcopal Dioceses of Delaware and Easton, Maryland; Fond du
Lac and Milwaukee, Wisconsin; Pennsylvania; and Spokane,
Washington
Episcopal Theological Seminary of the Southwest, Austin, Texas
The Lilly Summer Vocations Program, University of the South
Oregon Episcopal School and St. John the Baptist Church, Portland
St. Andrew's Cathedral in Jackson, Mississippi
St. Bartholomew's Church, Pittsboro, North Carolina
St. John's Cathedral, Denver, Colorado
St. John's Episcopal Church, Ellicott City, Maryland
St. Luke's Church in Ypsilanti, Michigan
St. Mark's Church, Richmond, Virginia
St. Paul of the Desert Episcopal Church, Palm Springs, California
St. Peter's Church, Charlotte, North Carolina
St. Stephen's Church, Schenectady, New York
Trinity Cathedral, Portland, Oregon
Trinity Church, Indianapolis, Indiana
Trinity Church, Martinsburg, West Virginia
Trinity Church Young Adults, New Orleans, Louisiana
Virginia Episcopal Theological Seminary, Alexandria, Virginia